# WONDERFUL WAYS
## _to_ BE _a_
# STEPPARENT

# WONDERFUL WAYS
## *to* BE *a*
# STEPPARENT

*Judy Ford* and *Anna Chase*

CONARI PRESS
Berkeley, California

*Cover illustration:* Lisa Burnett Bossi,
Fineline Marketing and Design

*Cover art direction:* Ame Beanland

*Cover and interior design:* Suzanne Albertson

Conari Press books are distributed by Publishers Group West.

ISBN: 1-57324-147-4

**Library of Congress Cataloging-in-Publication Data**
Ford, Judy.
Wonderful ways to be a stepparent / Judy Ford and Anna Chase.
p.     cm.
ISBN 1-57324-147-4 (tradepaper)
1. Stepparents.  2. Stepfamilies.  I. Chase, Anna.  II. Title.
HQ759.92.F67  1999                    98–44203
306.874—dc21                          CIP

Printed in the United States of America on recycled paper
99  00  01  02   RRD(C)  1  2  3  4  5  6  7  8  9  10

*Wonderful Ways to Be a Stepparent*

## DEALING WITH YOUR SPOUSE

## INTERACTING WITH THE KIDS

# *Acknowledgments*

Thanks to Alex Witchel, whose *Girls Only* gave us the inspiration for the unspoken "I Love You"s.

## FROM ANNA:

I want to give special thanks to Judy Ford for allowing me to share her "wonderful ways" format. I'd been searching for the right way to write about stepparenting for twenty years, and it wasn't until I saw her *Wonderful Ways to Love a Child* that I realized how to do it. Judy was gracious and generous enough to allow me to do this book with her.

Many conversations with stepparents and kids inform the pages of this book. I want to thank particularly Ann, Marilyn, Dawna, and Andy. I also want to thank, from the bottom of my heart, the angel, Daphne, who helped me through every stage and phase of the stepparenting process—I couldn't have done it without you.

Most of all, I want to thank my stepchildren, who appear in these pages as Michael and Zoe to protect their privacy. We have been in one another's lives now for twenty years, and much of who I am now is a result of the experiences we've had together. Thanks for being in my life.

## FROM JUDY:

I t is an enormously generous act by my daughter, Amanda, to allow me to write about her. I am eternally grateful for her presence in my life and in these pages.

I want to thank the many stepfamilies whom I've met in my parenting classes and as clients for the privilege of hammering out with them a new model for stepparenting.

And finally, my deepest appreciation to Conari Press, the publisher of all my books, for their ongoing commitment to my work.

# Once Upon a Time

The finest gift you can give
to your spouse and stepchildren
is the gift of gentle healing—
showing them that even after one family splits up,
you can *all* come together as an expanded clan.

You meet someone and fall in love—he's perfect in every way. Oh, and he has two kids from a former marriage who live with him half-time. No problem, you think. We love each other, so we can work out whatever issues the kids present. Right!

How many of us enter stepparenting totally blind, completely unaware of the pitfalls, problems, and difficulties ahead? Virtually all of us, we would venture to say. "I certainly was unaware of the challenges twenty years ago when a man and his two children, aged six months and two-and-a-half, came into my life," recalls Anna. "I remember thinking, 'Well, I like kids, so why not?' When we began to hit various bumps in the road—his son wanted nothing to do with me, his ex-wife broke into our house and destroyed my clothes—I was surprised. Shocked even. This was hard!"

No one can be prepared in advance for the roller coaster of experiences and emotions from all sides of blended families—yours, his, your kids, his kids, the in-laws, the ex-in-laws, the ex-spouse(s)....
Marriage and kids are hard enough, without adding the complexities of all those psyches, each potentially brewing up a batch of anger, resentment, and bitterness.

But stepparenting doesn't have to be all hell and hard work. Not that it isn't hard—(every single stepparent we spoke with admitted that the role was harder than they had expected)—but it can be easier with a bit of knowledge and a set of new attitudes. And sometimes, maybe often, maybe not, it can even be a source of joy and happiness. No matter what, it is always an opportunity for soul growth—yours, your spouse's, and the kids'. For, no matter how hard it gets, you are in their lives for a reason, as they are in yours.

"Twenty years ago, when I hit the skids of stepparenting," says Anna, "I sought advice in books, but didn't find anything truly useful. It was all too negative, or superficial and Pollyannaish. What you are holding in your hands now is the advice I wished I had then. It comes from two decades of my own experience and lots of conversations with other stepparents, combined with the positive 'parenting with love and laughter' approach of Judy Ford."

It is not our intention to sugarcoat the process of creating a blended family. But we do believe strongly that if you acknowledge the realities of the situation to yourself, your spouse, kids, and step-kids, and accentuate the positive on the day-to-day level, you can have a wonderful relationship with your stepchildren and live in a house full of love and laughter.

*Wonderful Ways to Be a Stepparent* is a prescription to strengthen your family. The book is filled with stories of stepparents who are building strong, loving new families, and offers more than sixty suggestions for dealing with everything from money and discipline to having more fun together. To really make these ideas work, you'll need compassion—for yourself, your spouse, and the children in your care—and all the emotional honesty you can muster.

To thrive, every child needs love, trust, respect, and acceptance, and the more adults who can provide these essential elements, the better. In the end, the labels *mother, father, stepmother, stepfather* matter less than the quality of our interactions with the young ones entrusted to our care. We stepparents have been give a precious opportunity to offer our love, trust, respect, and acceptance to the young souls who have entered our lives.

Stepparents are on a mission of hope and healing. When one family is separated by divorce or death, another family composition emerges. In time, the new family synthesis is often wiser, more compassionate, and rich with experience. It takes years to build a family history, years to have a happy ending, but it's worth the effort, because when you look back on your life together you'll discover it's chock-full of incredible human experiences. Your family history will be full of stories of healing, tears and laughter, and trials and triumphs that you'll all be retelling for years to come. These stories make you a family.

Stepparents arrive on the scene full of hope, bearing unspoken promises of fresh beginnings and renewal, promises of creating an expanded, richly textured family unit. By remembering this no matter what is happening, you will find that being a stepparent can be wonderful indeed, and that you can live happily together.

# RELATING TO YOURSELF

*The best reformers the world
has ever seen are those who
commence on themselves.*

—George Bernard Shaw

# OPEN YOUR HEART

Opening your heart to your stepchild may be very easy for you—or very difficult. It depends on the particulars of the situation and the personalities involved. But it is possible to do, even under the most trying circumstances, if you can engage your compassion.

Compassion is the ability to "feel with" someone else, to enter into his or her experience and recognize their pain. It's compassion we feel when we see a picture of children starving in Sudan and send money to CARE. It's compassion we experience when we notice a tired look on our beloved's face and offer to do the dishes.

We shouldn't be afraid of compassion for our stepchildren out of fear that they will "take advantage" of us. Rather, we should practice opening our hearts to them every day, if only in private, so that our compassion for their suffering can help us weather the rough spots in our relationship.

Everyone wants and needs to be loved—and that includes both you and the children who have come into your sphere of influence as a consequence of your relationship with their parent. You are probably aware of your desire for them to love, or at least have warm feelings, toward you. You want them to like you, to accept you, to treat you well, and to enjoy being in your company.

They, on the other hand, may be overtly needy of love, mouths wide open like baby birds waiting for worms, or as defensive and hostile as the most surly teenager is capable of. But don't let outward appearances fool you—no matter who your stepchild is, he or she longs to be known and appreciated. And no matter what situation you find yourself in, make no mistake in recognizing that your stepchild is as least as angry and scared as you—and with less experience in dealing with such strong feelings.

So there they are in front of you, with at *least* the intensity of emotions you are experiencing. They have not been on the Earth very long and have been through a lot already—the divorce or death of a parent; maybe several "potential stepparents" when Mom or Dad was dating; perhaps even a stepparent or two already. If we are willing to feel compassion toward these young souls, our hearts will naturally open as we empathetically relate to the suffering they have already gone through, the confusion they must be feeling right now. And when our hearts are open, our love will flow more freely—regardless of their ability to receive it in the moment.

# GIVE UP YOUR DREAM OF
# THE PERFECT FAMILY

Do you have an image of the perfect family? Chances are it comes from television. Depending on your age, it might be the Cleavers from *Leave It to Beaver*, the Keatons from *Family Ties*, or the Huxtables from *Cosby*. No matter which, these were all "intact" families with parents who loved each other well and communicated perfectly, and kids who, despite minor squabbles, got along heartwarmingly with one another and ultimately always took their parents' advice. These paragon families always celebrated Christmas and birthdays together, and went on happy family vacations.

In shape and substance, these media families probably bear little resemblance to the kind of family structure you now find yourself in. This can be hard. When we set ourselves up for a particular circumstance and it doesn't come to pass, we can get so focused on what we don't have that we can fail to appreciate what we do have. In particular, the nuclear family is a very potent archetype, which means it is locked into our deep unconscious as a model of how family life should be. When in reality we experience something different, there can be profound sadness or anger.

Rachel remembers how hard it was for her to come to terms with her new family. "For years, I constantly felt like the fifth wheel. The kids would arrive for a week, eager to see their dad. I was an afterthought. Whenever we would meet their friends, he would get introduced, but not me. I was irrelevant. And they never made me a Mother's Day card or gave me a birthday present. It was so painful, partly I guess because I had pictured us as *The Waltons* or something. When I finally stopped wishing it were different and made peace with the fact that we are a complex family that has a lot of issues to deal with, things got better. I stopped waiting for the birthday card and wishing for the Hallmark family moments, and lightened up. Miraculously, the kids felt the lack of pressure and actually got warmer toward me."

Your family is as unique as you are, and it is only because the Cleavers, the Huxtables, and the Keatons are fictional that their families are "perfect." Every family has its own difficulties and beauty. By giving up on an image of how it *should* be, you take a great step toward making it as good as it *can* be.

# DO A TWO-MINUTE REALITY CHECK

Remember the old adage—the truth will set you free? However you expected your family life to be before you got married, chances are your expectation doesn't match up to reality. That's why one of the first steps in making stepparenting wonderful is to let go of all the expectations of the way you thought it would—or should—be, and take a realistic look at the way things are. What this means is that either in a journal or a private conversation with yourself, take two minutes a day to do an inventory of the way things are. Not the way you wish they were or hope they could be, but what truly is: I'm having more trouble adjusting to life with kids than I thought I would; I'm angry Fred is feeling so guilty about the divorce that he is spoiling his kids and I'm afraid to talk to him about it; I'm hurt that little Emily is wary of me and Dylan is downright hostile.

It's really important that you just take note of the way things really are without judgment: I'm angry; I'm hurt; I'm feeling rejected. What's important about this judgment-free assessment is that it allows you to come out of denial and really face the truth of what's going on. This is not easy to do. Anna remembers that it took her a couple of years to admit that she was not happy about sharing her husband with her stepkids. "It just seemed so selfish and petty," she remembers. "I couldn't stand thinking of myself that way so that I kept pretending it wasn't true. But the more I pretended, the more angry and upset I got at myself, Bill, and his kids. It was only when I finally admitted to myself that I had negative feelings that I could begin to resolve them."

Take two minutes to make contact with reality: How do you feel about your role as a stepparent? About your stepkids, your spouse? Your living arrangements? And then comes the most important part— just sit with what is. Recognize the emotional truth of your situation— Oh, I'm hurt at getting no positive reinforcement from my stepchildren despite all I do for them; I'm angry at my wife's ex for not ponying up his share of the child support—and then hold it in the spaciousness of your consciousness for a quiet few minutes and go about your day. The next day, check in again with yourself—Yup, I'm still angry; I'm a bit less hurt cause Zoe smiled at me today—whatever's true for you.

This practice is about you accepting what is, not you blasting your ex or the kids or husband with what you've discovered. Maybe some day it will be appropriate to share—in loving language—some insight you've gained, but for the most part, the daily check-in is about you coming into the present moment. If you persist over time, chances are you will see how much your feelings, and the situation, change. Sometimes for the worse, but more likely, for the better, if only because your capacity to accept the way things are will have increased tenfold.

# BE REALISTIC ABOUT YOUR ROLE

We ask a lot of kids when we create blended families. No matter how old or young the child is, they already have a mother and a father, whom, for the most part, they still wish would live together. Then one (or both) parent asks that the child accept into their lives another parent (or two or three—we know several people who have had three stepmothers). The situation is not the child's doing; they have no choice in the matter. They must simply accept a new stepmother or father. No wonder they often create havoc for us.

The truth, of course, is that the child already has a mother and a father (even if the parents are dead or gone), and we can never fill that role, no matter how much we may care or try to. And no matter how much we try, they may never love us the way we would like to be loved. (Which doesn't mean we have to put up with bad behavior; they must treat us decently, as we would have them treat any other human being, no matter how they feel.)

Every single stepparent we spoke to for this book, no matter their circumstances, said the same thing—as long as they tried to be their stepchild's mother or father, and expected the love the "real" mother or father would receive, they were disappointed. But if they were willing to give up that particular parental role and listen for what the child really needed from them, they were able to forge a relationship that worked. And sometimes, it can develop into something as precious as parenthood.

"Bonnie's kids Lisa and Tim were eight and six when I came on the scene," remembers Tom. "Their father had abandoned Bonnie, but they were still resistant to my becoming their father. So I suggested they call me by my first name, which made them both a bit more comfortable. I kept my emotional distance, but became the all-around homework helper, and gradually I saw their respect and love grow. In high school, they both made contact with their father, but when it came time for Lisa to get married, while her father was there, it was me she wanted to have escort her down the aisle."

By not forcing our stepchildren to love us or see us as mother or father, we give them the emotional space they need to find their way to us.

# CREATE AN IDENTITY
# FOR YOURSELF

So if you can't take on the role of parent, who should you be? That is a question that only you can answer, depending on your personality, circumstances, the ages and personalities of your stepkids, and so on. But we do encourage you to create an identity for yourself and make it explicit to the kids. Humor really helps here.

Judy's life-partner Will always signed cards, notes, and presents to Judy's daughter Amanda: "From the man who ruined your childhood," which is what she claimed he had done. Sometimes she would scream, "I hate you! I hate you!" A couple hours or days later when the conflict had been long forgotten or resolved, Will would joke and laugh with Amanda, referring to himself as "the man you love to hate."

Through such humor, we tell our stepkids that we *are* in their lives, and that while we know they might not always be happy about that, we are an adult they must come to terms with. We also show that their feelings are not deadly, that it hasn't killed us that they said such a thing. This is important because children can get swamped by the strength of their feelings and believe they, as children, are omnipotent. When we make light of such remarks, they can see our sturdiness and rest in our strength.

Bridging the identity gap between how the children view you and how you'd like to be seen starts by receiving unpleasant news without freaking out. When Todd told his stepmom, "I don't like you," she kindly responded with, "You don't have to like me, if you choose not to, but I'm trying to like you." Peter told stepdaughter Amy, "I'm glad you can voice your negative feelings about me." By allowing her to do so, eventually she felt safe enough with him to share her anger toward her dad, with whom she didn't dare share her deep thoughts and feelings for fear he would abandon her completely.

Perhaps in the beginning your identity to the kids is that of an unwelcome intruder, but if you can be good-natured about it all, it can change from being an outsider to observer to being a sounding board and confidante. It depends on you. No one can step into a family and become an instant parent. If you can remember that your identity doesn't depend on what the kids call you or how they treat you, but rather on how you behave toward them, you'll be on the right track.

# MAKE PEACE WITH MINE
# VERSUS YOURS

Melanie raised seven children: three stepsons, two sons from her first marriage, and two children with her second husband. "Our house was a revolving door," she says. "We were the full spectrum: steps, halfs, and fulls, but we never referred to anyone as 'yours' or mine. They were all ours." When talking about one to the other it was, 'He's your brother, she's your sister.'

"We tried to keep the rules the same even if our sons were only with us part time, but it didn't always work out. Sometimes I thought my husband was too easy on his kids, other times he was convinced I was too hard on his and more lenient with mine. Then there were times when I was harder on mine and let his squeeze by."

While some experts might advise you to get over the "yours versus mine" attitude, don't worry if you can't get there. It may not be humanly possible. Your kids will always be yours; his kids will always be his. You bring to your union years of personal history which can't be wiped out so quickly. It's natural to have a unique love for your own child. Kids sense this and can cope with it better if you're honest about your tendencies.

Acknowledging that each parent prefers his or her own child is healthier than sweeping it under the rug. No need to get flustered, defensive, or contrary. The kids will respect your integrity and together you can finds ways to make up for the discrepancies. Admitting the inconsistencies works better than being hypervigilant to make sure every interaction is equal.

It also affects how stepsiblings get along. Joel brought his eight-year-old daughter, Molly, his bride Alyce, and ten-year-old step-daughter, Amelia, to counseling. Everything had been going smoothly until the wedding, when Molly suddenly withdrew, becoming more tearful and sullen each day. Joel was at a loss as to why things had changed. As Judy talked with them, Molly became more and more agitated and burst out, "I hate Amelia because my dad likes her just the same as me." It turns out that Joel had told the girls on the eve of the wedding, "From now on you're my girls—I love you the same." Molly was devastated, wondering how her father could love Amelia, whom he'd only know for a year, as much as he loved her.

Children need to know that they cannot be replaced so quickly in their parents' hearts. When you demote your child from the number-one position he once held, he feels emotionally abandoned, but when you tell him: "You're always number one in my heart," he can cope more easily with sharing you. Letting your child know that you will always love her and be there for her, above all else, can make a huge difference in your child's acceptance of stepsiblings.

# UNDERSTAND YOU'RE THE ADULT

Boy, is *this* a challenge. No matter what your parental status—parent or stepparent—there are times when all you want to do is to give in to the urge to scream, cry, hit, or throw yourself down on the ground like a two-year-old, pounding and kicking the floor.

And because of the complexities of stepparenting, the urge might strike quite a lot. Like when four-year-old Johnny, who is visiting for two months of summer vacation, screams at the top of his lungs in the store, "You're not my mom. I don't have to do what you say!" or Shelby announces in the middle of a business dinner party for twelve, "I hate you and wish you were dead." Or seven-year-old Samantha, in a fit of pique over your not allowing her to pierce her ears, threatens to move in permanently with her father and never show her face at your house again.

It's hard to resist walking out on Johnny in the store or saying "I hate you too, Shelby," or "Good, I'll be glad to get rid of you, Samantha," isn't it? Deep inside we have little selves the same age as Johnny and Shelby and Samantha and they have just gotten their feelings hurt. But one of the soul challenges that stepparenting continually calls us to face is to remember that we are now adults and as such have a responsibility to act more maturely than the beings in front of us. When we agreed to create this new family we took on an obligation to bring all our maturity to bear upon the situation and always to try to act for the highest good of the young ones in our care. This doesn't mean we will always succeed. We will lose our tempers and our tongues on occasion (for which we will later apologize). But in the heat of the moment, it's important to remember that the child in front of us who is acting so badly is at least as angry and hurt as we are (why else would they be saying such things?) and it is our job to figure out what he or she really needs.

Whatever situation you and your stepchildren are in—living together part-time, living together full-time and never seeing their other parent, visiting only on weekends or summer vacation, whatever—always remember that as tough as it is for you, it is that much harder for them. As children, they have fewer emotional resources and less control over the arrangements of their lives. If you remember that you are an adult and they are only children, it will make whatever negativity they fling in your direction easier to bear.

# FIND A SAFE HAVEN TO VENT

No matter how wonderful your family situation is, some times will be hard, horrible, even hellish, so be sure to have at least one friend who will listen sympathetically, offer support, and remind you of the worth of what you are doing.

"I've been fortunate to have a friend who started on the step-mother journey exactly at the same time as I did," says Anna. "She was the stepmother of three children who lived with her full-time, and I had two half-time. Neither of us had children of our own. We would talk frequently and at least once a year, we'd go away for a weekend of bitching, moaning, and complaining. It was great to discover that virtually everything I was experiencing she was also feeling. We would talk about feeling the pain of the undefined role—being ignored at high school graduation in favor of the 'real' parents, for example; our anger at the lack of privacy and intimacy with our spouse; our resentment over our increased workload—laundry and meals and car pools without receiving the kind of love the kids showered on their biological parents; and the financial strain and obligation we were forced to meet because of 'their' children. All the things we couldn't discuss with our mates because it would be too hurtful or with our other friends because they couldn't understand.

"We would commiserate with one another—it felt so good to be so totally understood—and somehow knowing that we weren't alone in feeling the way we did made it so much easier to keep on going."

Do you have someone you can pour out your heart to? It needs to be someone other than your mate. As loving and understanding as he or she might be, no one wants to hear what a drag their children are, and not many relationships can stand the burden of the kind of resentments that you might want to vent in the heat of the moment. Ideally, it would be another stepparent. If you don't have a good friend, consider joining a group or a stepparent chat room on the Internet. They should be easy to locate. But no matter where you look, be sure to find a sympathetic ear or two.

# BE READY FOR TOUGH QUESTIONS

"I will remember this day as long as I live," says Anna. "I was twenty-five years old, and suddenly found myself the stepmother of Michael, age two, and Zoe, age six months, who lived half the week with us and half the week with their mother. It was about six months into the creation of our new household, and we were sitting around eating dinner when three-year-old Michael looked straight at me (he had mostly ignored me to that point) and said, 'Why won't you let my dad come home?'

"I was stunned into silence as the enormity of the question and all its implications reverberated around me. How could I possibly explain to a three-year-old the complexities of adult emotional life? How could I deal with the fact that his mother had obviously blamed me for the situation and now he did too (not to mention that his remark revealed that 'home' to him was the other house, not where we lived)? I turned to his father for help; I can't remember what he said in response.

"I know I said nothing and even now, twenty years later, I regret that. If only someone had taken me aside beforehand and said, 'This is going to be hard. It's going to be hard on you and even harder on the kids. Be ready for tough questions. If you don't know what to say, tell them their question matters to you and you are going to think about it. Then get advice—from a therapist, an experienced friend, a book.'"

And so now, this is our advice to you—be prepared for the unexpected: the tough question, the difficult situation. By being emotionally prepared, you can gather the resources you need when the time comes.

# ACKNOWLEDGE YOUR
# FEELINGS OF JEALOUSY

I spent years resenting the amount of time my husband spent with his kids, and they resented the time he spent with me, I discovered recently from my stepdaughter," says Marie, a stepmother of two children. "For several years they lived three hundred miles away and Don would drive down to see them for the weekend at least once a month. I was lonely and blamed the kids for my situation. Even when I would go or they would come to our house, I felt as though I was irrelevant. They had a mom and a dad and were not interested in a relationship with me. Even though they didn't live with us full-time, I felt like the three of them were a family and I was an outsider. Perhaps if I had had a child of my own the feeling would not have been so strong."

Fred, on the other hand, was extremely jealous of Cynthia's previous husband, Walter. Her kids were a constant reminder that she had loved another man, and because they shared custody, Cynthia saw Walter frequently, which drove Fred up the wall.

Many times in divorce situations, stepparents feel jealous—of the ex-spouse, the time and attention the children get, the money that gets spent on the stepkids, the fact that the spouse has children and you do not. In stepfamilies, there are a myriad of ways to feel jealous and excluded. Again, the trick is first to acknowledge the truth of how you feel: for example, "Yes, I am jealous every time Don goes over to Sue's house to get the kids." Sit with the truth of how you feel without judgment, without trying to fix it or change it—"Yup, there it is, jealousy again. Yup."

By sitting quietly with it, the feeling may begin to shift. If it doesn't, you might want to find a time to talk over the issue with your mate. Choose a good time (not when he's got one foot out the door to Sue's house!) and quietly verbalize your feelings. Perhaps verbalizing them and hearing his or her assurances is all you need. Or maybe together you can come up with a solution that can accommodate everyone: Don will ask the kids to meet him in the front yard, for instance.

The trick is to acknowledge your true feelings, discover whether something has to be done about them and then present the situation in as nonconfrontational a manner as possible. (And go easy on yourself if you don't do this perfectly—it's hard!)

# DON'T EXPECT TO BE
# THANKED OVERTLY

There's an old saying that parenting is a thankless task, but it's an understatement where stepparenting is concerned. After all, especially when they are little, kids are generally loving and sweet toward their parents—kissing, hugging, bringing them pictures and presents they made in school. But with stepparents, it's the third-wheel problem again. You are often perceived to be an extraneous or even unwanted addition. And the stepchildren might feel very disloyal about showing you appreciation or affection, particularly if the ex has vilified you. No wonder they don't thank you for being in their lives.

"I was highly sensitive to this issue," says Francine, a mother of two and stepmother of two. "Every Mother's Day, my kids made me cards, but there was never anything from my stepkids. I felt unrecognized and unappreciated for all the work I do—cooking, cleaning, shlepping. . . . I started to dread the day. It reminded me that my stepkids never say 'I love you' to me either and that hurts a lot too."

There are no easy answers to such hurt. But one possible balm is to give up any expectations (expectations *always* cause angst because no one can live up to anyone else's), but live with expectancy—which is an openness to something positive happening. Francine hasn't gotten a Mother's Day card yet, but three years into her role as a stepmother, her stepdaughter Kate said to her one day, "I love the way you make chocolate chip cookies and put a special message inside my lunch bag. All the other kids at school are jealous." Because she kept her heart open and offered loving care to her stepchildren without expecting gratitude, she received the thanks she so richly deserved.

# ALWAYS REMEMBER YOUR STEPCHILDREN LOVE THEIR OTHER PARENT

Depending on your circumstances, this may take emotional and spiritual maturity. "Bill had the ex-wife from hell, and she had her guns trained on me," remembers Anna. "She blamed me for the divorce and acted out in all kinds of ways—she broke into our house and destroyed my clothes, she called hundreds of times a day and hung on the phone not speaking. Every time Bill went to drop off the kids after the weekend, they fought. We finally had to get an unlisted phone number and designate a friend as the number she could call in case of emergency, and enlisted mutual friends to be the go-betweens for kid transfers. Even after years passed and tempers cooled somewhat, she refused to ever be in the same room with me and still has never spoken to me.

"Nonetheless, the kids never heard a bad word pass my lips about their mother. I vowed to myself that I would never put them in the position of feeling disloyal to her or feeling guilty about loving her. Whenever something painful to me would come up—that I was banned from eighth-grade graduation or the tennis tournament, say—rather than exploding, I would try and remember that their mother was a soul just as I was, trying the best she could, and that it was her woundedness that was causing her to act the way she did. She never knew me; my attempts at understanding and acceptance were all private. But I know in my heart that my stepkids, spouse, and I all benefited from my silently sending love rather than hate, peace rather than enmity."

As Joyce and Barry Vissell say in their wonderful book *Models of Love*, "On some level children must all feel that they are a deep part of both their mother and their father. When a mother [or stepmother] complains to her son about his father, the child feels she is also attacking him. In their childlike simplicity they reason, 'You think my daddy is no good. Since I'm a part of daddy, you must feel I am no good too.'" Don't play bash the ex; let your stepkids have their loving feelings unconflictedly.

# GET A DIPLOMA IN DIPLOMACY

Do we stepparents need this one! We need it when our stepkids are waxing eloquently about their "real" father, whom we know is a drunk who abused them and their mother, or when they tell us all about their wonderful mother, whom we know to be a narcissistic hysteric who couldn't love a child if you gave her a million dollars to do it. We have to remember that these are our stepchildren's parents, and it is not our job to disillusion them (most likely they will see the truth as young adults on their own; coming to terms with their parents is a job only they can do). If you're tempted to try, it's helpful to remember that all that is likely to happen is that they will end up hating *you* for badmouthing their beloved.

So what do you say that is honest and not hurtful? "This is where the diplomacy degree comes in," says Anna. "What I used to say was something simple like, 'I'm glad you love your mother.' Or 'It's great that you have so many people who love you.' That way I neither affirmed nor disagreed with what they were saying, but responded to the emotional need I thought they were expressing."

The diplomacy degree comes in handy almost daily: when seven-year-old Chloe shows up from her mother's with makeup on and mother's approval; when fourteen-year-old Josh brings the "cool gun" his father bought him into your pacifist household. You have to negotiate these tricky waters without denigrating the other parent, for the more you rail against the bad judgment, character, or habits of the ex-spouse, the more you drive your stepchild away from you and into the other parent's arms.

This is particularly tricky if the other person is dead. We have a friend who married a widower with three kids. "Try competing with a dead mother," bemoans Shirley. "She has become a saint in their minds because she is no longer around to disappoint and fail them as all parents do. Everything I do is compared to the fantasized behavior of this paragon of love."

No matter what your situation, badmouthing the ex is the quickest way to disaster. You don't have to like her, you don't have to let the gun he gave Josh into your house, but if you want a happy relationship with your stepchildren, you do have to figure out how to speak pleasantly of their other parent.

# LIGHTEN UP

Recently we read a Miss Manners column in which a single parent described being hurt by her fiancé's child's comment. On the way to a video arcade with both sets of kids, Junior piped up with something like, "I wish it were just you and me, Dad, and nobody else going to play." The writer was expressing hurt and anger that her fiancé did nothing to "correct" Junior's behavior.

If this woman was upset enough to write to Miss Manners about Junior, she is in for a rough ride as a stepmother! Of course Junior said it on purpose to hurt her feelings and will continue to say such things (and much worse!) if he gets the reaction he wants—which is to create distance, division, and discord so that (he hopes) she and her kids will go away.

In such circumstances, what works best is to lighten up and not take such comments too seriously. A simple lighthearted, "Oh yes, it's nice to do things alone with your father sometimes, but today we're all playing together" would have sufficed. If you can think of a witty repartee, that is even better. Or ignore the comment altogether and challenge him to a one-on-one game of Mario Cart or Double 007 Golden Eye.

If you have children of your own who are also being snubbed, be sure to talk to them privately about the situation later: "Did Junior hurt your feelings? He's mad about sharing time with his dad. It's not personal."

Treat such "barbs" lightly and they will diminish over time. Take them too seriously and you will spend a great deal of time being hurt.

# GO EASY ON YOURSELF

Stepparenting is tricky business and you are not always going to do it right. So while you are being understanding and tolerant toward the difficulties your stepchildren face, be sure to give yourself the same amount of compassion. You will say or do the wrong thing sometimes. You will have negative thoughts toward your mate and stepkids. As long as you sincerely apologize for anything you verbalize, you don't need to wallow in guilt. In fact, it is counterproductive.

"For the longest time I used to feel guilty because I didn't love my stepkids the way my husband did," recalls Anna. "I hated myself for not loving them, I hated them because their presence was a constant reminder of my lack of loving feelings, and I hated my husband for 'getting' me into the mess in the first place. As long as I expected to have the same warm and fuzzy feelings as Bill did, I could not be open to the positive feelings I did experience toward them. When I stopped 'shoulding,' I began to go easier on myself and then was able to go easier on them. These days, as my stepdaughter reaches her late teens, she gets along much better with me than she does with her father, who 'loves' her more than I do."

We know lots of stepparents who love their stepkids, and virtually every one of them would admit that it is not exactly in the same way as a parent loves his or her child. That might not be all bad;

parental love can be so ego-involved that we try to get our kids to live out our unfulfilled dreams. As stepparents, we have less ego involvement and therefore perhaps more ability to see our stepchildren for the unique souls they are. As long as we hold their highest good foremost in our hearts as we interact with them, we will have done our job well.

So go easy on yourself when you feel frustrated, cranky, or unloving. You are doing the best you can and chances are that's very good indeed.

# CHERISH THE ABSURD

Let's be brutally honest here: Marrying someone doesn't automatically make you a parent. Oh yes, you act like a parent because of all the stuff you're doing. You might even be doing the job brilliantly but still you aren't entitled to the position until you've earned it. The privilege of being a parent to someone else's children is earned through considerable pain and sacrifice. Just as a woman gives birth following bouts of morning sickness, stretch marks, bloating, and excruciating labor pains, so too will you become a stepmother or a stepfather only after enduring substantial torture and testing. To be a parent you must first survive the initiation. And as you've found out by now there's plenty of hazing to endure. Don't take it personally; it's the path each stepparent walks.

Let's face it—you had no way of knowing when you married the "love of your life with the adorable little kids" what you were signing up for. Becoming a blended family is complex; after all, you're dealing with family history that you had no part in writing.

When two families come together there are bound to be competition and jealousy, rejection and anger. Each family is a multidimensional system with its own peculiar operating procedures, and there's mounds of confusion to climb over when you put them together. For example, Claire was dumbfounded when her surly ten-year-old stepson answered her request to take off his muddy shoes, "You're not my mother, you can't make me!" This was followed by, "Will you make us tacos for lunch?"

The more difficult your situation, the more you need laughter. Without a sense of the ridiculous and a well-developed appreciation of the absurd, the rough spots will split into caverns. According to the Stepfamily Association of America, it takes five to seven years for an expanded family with young stepchildren to reach some stability. If a teenager is involved, it may never happen.

As a stepparent, you'll have to develop the knack of stepping back, letting go, and observing the goings on around you. Make no mistake about it—while you're being ignored, you're being watched and tested. The harder you try to assume the role of new parent, the harder the children will resist; the less you try to take over, the better the chances for happiness. It's true, you can't become an instant parent, but while you're cooking the meals and doing the laundry you can finely tune your sense of the inane.

# GIVE YOURSELF CREDIT FOR
# A JOB WELL DONE

Do you focus on what you've done well as a stepparent, or do you only dwell on the negative? One way to make the experience as positive as possible is to do a little one-minute inventory at the end of the day (or whenever the kids are around): I like the way I handled the situation with Ben when he was so upset at himself for losing the tennis match; I did well on the phone with Martha's ex; John and I did well not to get pulled into our kids' fight with one another—for a change they actually worked it out well.

By focusing on the positive—we're doing a pretty good job—we give our psyches a boost, which makes it easier to keep on going. Noticing what's right also trains the brain to respond that way when a similar situation comes up again. It also allows our mind to think about ways to adapt what's working to other situations. When we focus on the negative, all we tell ourselves is that we don't know what we're doing and we get disheartened. Our creative thinking shuts down and our options of response dwindle. If all we notice is that we yelled, the next time all we will know how to do is yell—and then feel more guilty that we haven't stopped yelling.

So appreciate yourself today for all that you have done right as a stepparent! Get yourself a package of gold stars and award then to yourself. Tell a friend three things you're proud of as a stepparent today. Remember—It's not just "idle" praise. The more you focus on the positive, the more you will remember to do well in the future.

# KNOW YOU'RE NOT ALONE

For most stepparents, the process of being involved with someone else's children is not a walk in the park. Sometimes, when you are tempted to sink into despair and take the situation too personally, it really helps to remember that you are not alone in facing difficulties. In other words, it's not a personal failing on your part that is making stepparenting challenging or downright difficult—it just is hard, at least some of the time.

It's hard not to take an adolescent boy's silent animosity or a girl's acting out toward you personally—after all, they are persons who are directing their sullenness or open anger directly at you. But if you can remember that millions of people, both kids and adults, are struggling with the exact same issues, it can help you to depersonalize the situation a bit. From the distance that depersonalizing creates, you can perhaps regain your lightheartedness and good humor.

"I remember once when Michael was going through a particularly surly teenage phase and his father was working 'round the clock, and I was feeling resentful that I had to care for such a nasty and ungrateful stepchild," says Anna. "I went around in a huff for days, but finally decided that perhaps I could break the mood with a little humor. So the next day, when he was arguing with me over whether the sky was truly blue (honest!), I said with humor in my tone, 'I know it's your job as a teenager to disagree with whatever an adult says and particularly with me, but could you take a vacation from your job for the rest of the evening?' I can't say that he actually laughed, but he did lighten up and treated me well the rest of the day."

One excellent way to remember that you are not alone is to join a support group. It's great to have folks to commiserate with, and maybe other people will offer creative solutions to situations that have stalemated you. If you don't know of any existing groups, go ahead and make one of your own. We suggest you hold meetings away from prying ears and eyes so that you feel free to express your emotional truth. One word of caution—commiserating is one thing, but getting caught forever in a cycle of negativity toward exes and stepkids is another. Make a commitment in your group to focus on positive solutions and to help one another seek the good and avoid wallowing in bitterness and anger.

# REMEMBER YOU CHOSE THIS

When things get rough, it's important to remember that you chose this relationship in the first place. You fell in love with a person who had children, and you agreed to accept the children into the new family you are creating. You may secretly wish he didn't have kids; you may hope that she doesn't get custody, but the truth is when you get involved with a person with kids, you are taking on the new identity of stepparent even if at this moment the kids aren't on the scene. You can do it willingly or kicking and screaming, but *you are choosing to do it.*

"For the longest time, I saw myself as a person in love with Bill, a man who just *happened* to have two children who lived with him half-time," says Anna. "I glossed over the fact that his kids were a huge part of his life and in making a commitment to him, I had to make a commitment to his children as well. I didn't want it to be true, so I pretended it wasn't, even though the kids were there every Friday through Sunday.

"Finally I realized—I had *chosen* this situation. Even though I did not consciously choose, even though up till then I would have denied I chose, the fact was I had. It wasn't a 'coincidence' that Bill had kids. It was part of what I was signing up for. And it was perfect for me— I was able to parent without being 'the mother,' which, as the daughter of a very difficult alcoholic mother, was too scary for me. This way I could do it without having the full burden of the role."

Anna is friends with a couple who each had two kids, ages eight and ten. When the couple married, her kids lived with them and his kids lived with his ex-wife. Then his ex-wife was murdered, and suddenly they had four kids under one roof. It was difficult, to say the least. The kids were in open warfare with one another, and two were grieving the death of their mother. The couple could easily say that they had not chosen this particular situation.

True, but when they meet and decided to marry, they did know that there were four kids. And given the vagaries of life—death, changing custody arrangements particularly as children get older and express preferences—they knew somewhere in themselves that they were at least potentially taking on the responsibility of the whole brood. Unfortunately, this couple did not see their choice in the situation. As a consequence, they remained bitter and angry, and their children, now in their thirties, are all estranged from them and from one another.

We may have chosen consciously or unconsciously, but we have agreed to participate in this new configuration. If we can feel our choosing and look for the underlying positive reasons for our choice, it will make the day-to-day easier.

# SEARCH FOR THE SOUL GROWTH

Each and every one of us is here on Earth to grow our souls, to become the best of who we can be, love as well as we can, and offer our unique gifts to the world. To do these tasks well, we need to be constantly asking ourselves as we navigate the whitewater rapids of life: What is being asked of me here in terms of soul growth? Am I being called to be more forgiving? Less angry? More receptive? Less fearful?

All of life is a school for the soul, a series of "classes" in which we are called upon to learn the lessons and move to the next level. Seen in this light, all of our challenges—whether they have to do with our health, relationships, or work—are opportunities to grow our souls bigger and wider and to live more fully and deeply. In this sense, those of us who are stepparents have been given the special opportunity to grow our souls through the experience of interacting with and helping to *care for and guide* someone else's children.

To live with this awareness at the forefront of our minds is to change dramatically our relationship to the challenges of stepparenting. Rather than dwelling on the negatives—I can't get any respect, the ex-wife is driving me insane, the kids are wild when they come back from a weekend with Dad—this perspective asks us to discover what each challenge is calling for in terms of our soul development.

Is it more tolerance? Less selfishness? More compassion or patience? A willingness to let go of a grudge?

Ellen, whose parents were killed when she was eight years old, grew up being shuffled from one relative to another. An only child, lonely and isolated, she escaped into books and her studies. Secretly she longed for brothers and sisters and prayed every day that she would some day have a family. In her mid-thirties, she fell in love with and married David, a widower with three small children. She knew this family was the answer to her prayers, and she happily gave up her career to become a wife and a mother.

Thus began the difficult task of healing. When seven-year-old Lindsey cried, "I want my mommy in heaven, not you," Ellen was shaken to her soul. She hadn't cried when her own mother died twenty-nine years before, and she didn't know how to comfort Lindsey. For months, she withdrew into books and thought about leaving, but fortunately she didn't. If she was to discover her soul lessons, this was indeed the perfect family in which to do it.

No matter what the particulars of your situation, you are enrolled in stepparenting school and the object of the learning is to become the most loving, wise, compassionate self that you are capable of being. To be willing always to look for the lesson is to imbue your role with the highest mission and receive from it the highest reward.

# DEALING WITH YOUR SPOUSE

*The meeting of two persons'*
*abilities is like the contact of two*
*chemical substances: if there is any*
*reaction, both are transformed.*

—Carl Jung

# TALK, TALK, TALK
# TO YOUR PARTNER

Good communication is a hallmark of any healthy relationship, and nowhere is it more necessary than between the adults who live in a family with stepchildren. Probably you did a tremendous amount of talking *before* you made the commitment to live together, and you have some mutually agreed-upon principles regarding the children in your life. But love is often blind, even the second or third time around, so perhaps you didn't fully explore the kinds of issues you are now facing. In either case, life has a way of throwing curveballs at us, so that chances are even if you did discuss parenting, you are encountering situations you never dreamed possible.

That's why it's so important to keep on talking to one another about what is going on—how you both are feeling, what you think the kids might be needing, how to handle the request for a change in the custody arrangements. And be sure to do it in private, so that the kids are protected from your uncensored remarks. ("One of the advantages of joint custody," notes Anna, "is it gives you time alone. Of course you end up using a lot of it talking about the kids.")

Be very careful about how you communicate your negative feelings or impressions to your mate. Remember he or she loves their child very much and might get defensive if you appear to be on the attack. If you, with a more objective eye, see something that needs addressing, be sure to choose the time and your words carefully or your comments could backfire on you.

"When Bill and I first started living together, he felt very guilty about the divorce's effect on his three-year-old son Michael. So he was hesitant to discipline him at all and Michael was running wild. I hung back for a few weeks, waiting to see what would happen and feeling it was not my place, at least not yet, to discipline Michael. Finally I said something to Bill. He admitted that his guilt was holding him back from doing the right thing. Then he said that he was going to take Michael on a week's vacation alone, so that Michael could feel Bill's love and receive some undivided attention. When they returned, he would be willing to start enforcing the rules. Well, Bill stuck to his word and we had a few rocky days as Michael rebelled against the new regime. I know that if I had said something sooner, Bill would not have been ready to hear me."

Sometimes feelings get so volatile that good communication between you is not possible. If you find yourself in that place, please seek out professional help—a minister, a therapist. He or she can help you find a bridge back to one another.

# BREAK THE MOLD AND DESIGN A NEW MODEL

I f you only remember one thing about the process of becoming a blended family, remember this: You can't instantly take over the parenting functions for children who are not your own. When Judy sees blended families in her family counseling practice, she asks the children what kind of relationship they would like to have with their parent's new wife or husband. "In all the years I've been asking this question I have never had a child answer, 'I'd like her to be a mother to me,' or 'I'd like him to be another father.'"

Children are not looking for another parent—even if one of their parents has died. What they do wish for is a friendly relationship. They'd like the new spouse to be like a special coach or helpful teacher, a confidante, a grown-up buddy, a mentor. They want their parents to treat all the children and each other well. They wish for harmony, courtesy, and respect between *all* the adults, including exes.

The blended families Judy has worked with who have been able to accomplish a harmonious family life have done so by first breaking out of the stereotypical mold of what a stepmother or stepfather is suppose to be and do, and have started from scratch. Instead of trying to look like a traditional nuclear family, they have carved out a new model for their expanded family.

To create a harmonious blended family, you don't have to function like the nuclear family you grew up in. In a blended family it works best if the biological parent continues to be responsible for the parenting of his or her own children. Traditionally, when Dad remarries, bringing children to the new household, he turns the parenting over to Stepmom, then more or less withdraws. This old model keeps the new spouse locked in the "wicked stepmother" position. Instead of living on the outskirts of family life, the biological parent must stay active in all aspects of parenting and family life. When the biological parent steps up to his or her parenting obligations, the new spouse gets the luxury of relaxed time with the children, and their relationship develops in a more satisfying direction.

Tim has custody of his three children, ages seven, nine, and ten. When Sarah, his fiancée, moved in and assumed the role of mother, family life deteriorated rapidly. In desperation, they came to counseling and constructed a model for their family that had greater potential for success. The first change made was that Sarah relinquished the mother role and went to work full-time. Tim cut his overtime work hours and took back the "mother and father" role he had assumed for the previous three years. Sarah once again could relate to the kids as the family friend. Everyone was happier and the wedding date was set. Now, after three years of marriage, the kids call her "Our Sarah."

# BE GOOD HOUSEMATES

Here's a bit of advice from Elizabeth, who lives with her husband Don and four teenage stepsons: "Don't get caught up on the word *family*. Family is a concept with so much emotional charge behind it that trying to turn your household into one can bog you down with unruly expectations."

"We call ourselves 'five bachelors and a babe,'" said Don, who recognized early on that his boys, whom he had raised for six years by himself, were not about to accept Elizabeth as mother. "I didn't have a clue how to live with spirited testosterone-charged young men," said Elizabeth, "so instead of mothering them we work on becoming good housemates." Don agrees, "In many ways we're closer than most families I see, yet that's not how we describe ourselves."

Whether you call yourself a tribe, a clan, kindred souls, housemates, or enemies living under one roof, it doesn't matter as much as your attitude. With a little imagination, you can come up with a title that describes your state of affairs in a fresh and lively way.

Begin by brainstorming a description or title for your group. Think of your living situation as a television sitcom—what title can you give it that would draw the largest audience? Think of a title that will make the other members of the group sit up and take notice. In a stepparenting class, one family decided to call themselves, "The Brady

Bunch Goes to War"; another called themselves, "The Mighty Six."

By thinking of yourself as housemates you remove the authoritarian edge and move more easily into collaboration. "We've ground out housemate policies for everything from where to keep the boys' cereal to 'hands off' signs on my private shelf in the cupboard," says Elizabeth. "They teach me 'guy stuff' like how to ride dirt bikes and spit; I teach them to take their shoes off in the house, and to appreciate flowers and candles, and other 'girlie' stuff."

In describing your living arrangements and in making housemate policies, begin where you are, not where you think you should be. If you're joining forces, for example, with a bunch of boys who have never sat a table for dinner, you can't expect to have formal dining off the bat. Begin by making a proposal to eat around a table one night a week. Enlist their cooperation by pleading, bribing, and begging if you must—but no nagging or threatening.

Keep the discussions on houschold policies lively by joking, being silly, and exaggerating the obvious. "Okay, let's live as dirty slobs for one week," said one stepmother, while trying to establish household procedures for the laundry room. When you think of your group as a sitcom and your housemates as cast members you take the pressure off. There's no need to create a happily-ever-after ending. All you need is for each episode to be entertaining.

# MERGE YOUR PARENTING STYLES

T he best thing about Bill's and my parenting styles," recalls Anna, "is that we almost never disagreed. We really had very similar philosophies that, moment to moment, translated into a style in which it was very easy to back one another up. So I was never pitted against the kids and Bill. In a disagreement, we stood together." But what if the two of you don't have a natural stylistic affinity or, as can happen, you believe your spouse is just plain wrong sometimes?

Kids sense when parents have different styles; they know who is the more lenient, for example, and who is stricter. And they will use that knowledge if you don't figure out a way to create at least a smidgen of unity. "Yes, Dad wants you to do the dishes immediately following dinner. So right now, please do it his way. Let's talk it over with him later and perhaps tomorrow we can try another way." Talking about your parenting differences in this way builds on your relationship with the kids while teaching respect for the other parent's ways. It shows them that you can work together even though you have differences.

Merge your styles by trying out each other's ways, and enlist the kids to participate in the process. Dad thinks we should do it this way, Mom thinks this way might work better. Ask the kids if they have a compromise. The Bensons were a blended family with some kids living with them full-time and others coming for weekends and extended holidays. One side of the family was easygoing about household habits and rules; the other side were clean fanatics and preferred a firm set of operating procedures. The complicated merger was achieved by enlisting everyone's input. The kids surprisingly came up with the solution: three slogans—"Cleanliness is harder, but better," "Treat each other respectfully," and "Negotiate the rest"—became their working philosophy. Involving the kids in the solutions places the emphasis on teamwork and cooperation rather than pitting parents against kids.

If your children are able to come between you to divide and conquer, you and your spouse may have unresolved parenting issues. If this is happening, you may need to write down a list of house rules that you both can agree to: bedtime at 8:00; no sweets till after dinner. When you are in agreement, you will be able to back each other up without giving mixed messages to the kids. The time you spend talking this over with each other will also help you find your merged parenting style.

So many kids of divorce have to deal with different rules at Mom's and Dad's. If the two of you are in harmony, that makes at least one place of solid ground for the kids to stand on.

# DEAL WITH DISCIPLINE

Nowhere is a merger of parenting philosophy more vital than in the area of discipline. What we mean here is that you and your spouse have to be in agreement with what is worth holding the line for, and how you are going to do it. Are the two of you going to enforce the rules with the kids, or are you as the stepparent going to hold back and let the biological parent take the lead?

No one can tell the two of you what to do or exactly how to do it, for particularly in blended families, it all depends on the circumstances. If you are parenting very young children who spend a great deal of time with you, it is probably best if you both establish yourselves as authority figures. But if you are a newcomer to the scene encountering a surly twelve-year-old whom you see only for a week at Christmas vacation, you might want to take a different tack than head-to-head confrontation to establish your authority.

In either case, you and your spouse need to talk about discipline and consequences—at best before the kids arrive, but if not, as soon after as possible. What are your ground rules? How have you dealt with disobedience in the past? How comfortable are your stepkids with you? How do you feel about your spouse telling your children what to do? These are all considerations in establishing the whats and hows of discipline.

So many stepparents disapprove of the way their spouse handles his or her children but are afraid to say anything. Unless the two of you can agree on a strategy—even if the strategy is that you, the stepparent, will stay out of it—there will be discord between you, and that will spill over into your lives with the kids. A discipline strategy that you both agree upon—a time-out for the offending child with conversation afterward to discuss the misbehavior, enforced by whoever was witness to the event, for example—will go a long way toward creating harmony at least between the two of you. When you believe that you will stand together and support the strategy you have created, you feel a strong, loving connection to your spouse, even when the kids are misbehaving. But if you don't have that unity, find yourselves fighting between yourselves, as well as with the children in your care.

# RIDE OUT THE
# COMPLEXITIES TOGETHER

" This one took me a long time to learn," remembers Anna. "When things got tough, I used to set Bill up as the villain, throwing things in his face like 'These are your ex-wife and your kids and it's all your fault that we are in this awful situation!' He would always say, 'I'm not the enemy. I'm on your side, trying to figure out the best thing to do for all of us.' I desperately wanted to blame someone, and he was the most convenient target. Needless to say, it was very destructive to our relationship. Even now, if things get really heated with one of the kids, I still have that tendency. But I've learned to try and breathe quietly and say to myself over and over, 'He's not the enemy. We can work this out together.'"

Blaming is a wonderfully easy relationship sinkhole, and it's particularly common for stepfamilies to fall into it. After all, at any given moment, it's the other person's kids (or ex) causing a ruckus. Why shouldn't he or she pay by being on the receiving end of our totally righteous anger?

Unless you want to end up in divorce court (again), avoid the blame sinkhole at all costs. Regardless of whose kids they are legally, by virtue of you and your spouse's commitment to one another, you are in this together, and together you need to find the way out.

This togetherness extends to all aspects of your lives. Whether it is simply trying to figure out the arrangements for getting two kids to soccer practice and one to piano lessons after school or negotiating a delicate peace between two children who are less than happy about being "blended," you need both your energies, commitment, and cooperation. If you want your relationship to thrive, there can be no room for "That's your problem because it's your kid," or "You deal with it because you created the mess in the first place." Come together and you won't have to come apart.

# LAUGH TOGETHER (A LOT)

I sn't laughter great? Laughter dispels tension, defuses anger, dilutes hostility. It's particularly wonderful for creating intimacy in a relationship, a private space between you and your mate where you acknowledge the humor in whatever is going on. Laughter bonds you together, which is particularly handy when the situation is threatening to tear you apart.

"I will never forget the day we had sent four-year-old Zoe to her room for a time-out," says Anna. "She was screaming and crying, 'I want my mom,' which she routinely did whenever Bill or I disciplined her. That always set my nerves on edge—I felt guilty about the situation and angry that she would hurt me by throwing her mother in my face. She wailed for a long time. Then we noticed there were longer and longer intervals between the wails, and they were losing intensity: Waah! Waah. Silence. Silence. Silence. *Waah*.... *Waah*. We snuck up to her room and peeked in the doorway. There she was, happily coloring away, until she would remember that she was supposed to be upset and let out a couple wails for our benefit. We snuck back downstairs and laughed together until our sides ached. We still laugh about it—sixteen years later."

Will asked seven-year-old Amanda how she would like to introduce him. She shrugged her shoulders, seemingly not to care. Will continued with the line of questioning, listing a number of options: "How about as your mother's friend, as your uncle, a family acquaintance, Mom's boyfriend, neighbor, stepdad?" Amanda continued ignoring him. Finally Will asked again, "How do you want to introduce me when your friends come over?" Amanda quietly answered, "As my mom's ex-boyfriend!" "We roared until tears were streaming down our cheeks." For the next seven years of Will's life, whenever Judy and Will had a tiff they'd tease each other and say, "Watch out or I'll introduce you as my ex."

Practice laughing with each other and smiling. At the end of the day, when you are alone, share a story about the funny things the kids said or did. Laugh about the insanity of it all. Your spouse will appreciate you so much if you can get into the habit of seeing the funny side of your situation. Laughter is the aphrodisiac your relationship needs to withstand the pulls that stepparenting will inevitably bring.

# ACKNOWLEDGE
# YOUR BOUNDARIES

Everyone, no matter how spiritually and emotionally mature, has limits. In fact, boundaries are healthy—when they serve to protect us from harm and do not limit our soul growth. When dealing with stepkids, it's important to acknowledge to your partner—in a loving way of course—where your limits are.

"Because of the rough start with Bill's ex-wife," says Anna, "I became very fearful of her. I was afraid of her anger toward me, and of her anger toward the kids as a consequence of their relationship with me. So one of my boundaries was that I would not do the kid transfers. No matter how hard I tried, I was just too afraid of her volatility to even consider it. It was a relief when the kids got old enough to take public transportation and could go back and forth on their own. I wish I could have come to the place where I could let go of my fear, but I never have."

There's a big difference between acknowledging boundaries and refusing to participate because "they're your kids." The first is a sincere, heartfelt acknowledgment that some of what needs to be done is just not possible for you to do right now. The other is an angry, resentful refusal to participate in the process. The first invites closeness; the second is a slap in the face.

Only you can know where your boundaries are, and only your spouse can report in on her or his own limits. Are there areas in your life where you feel put upon? Chores or activities that you feel resentful about doing? Make a list of things you don't like doing. Don't leave anything out. Put your list aside for a day or two and then read it over, placing a star by the three most urgent items. Ask your spouse to do the same. After your lists are complete, set aside a time in a neutral place, such as your favorite coffee shop, to go over your lists. See if together you can find a solution so that the starred items can be eliminated, made easier, or handled in a better way.

Otherwise, your relationship will suffer because you'll start withdrawing from each other. Remember: 60 percent of second marriages end in divorce because conflicts and resentments aren't resolved. The time you spend resolving the conflicts and setting your boundaries will help keep your relationship thriving.

# SAY SOMETHING POSITIVE
# ABOUT THE OTHER PARENT

One of the biggest hazards to a harmonious stepfamily is ongoing conflict with an ex-spouse. For children to make a positive adjustment following divorce and remarriage, they need a loving relationship with both parents. That means you must never criticize, put down, badmouth, or gossip about the other parent. You must not stand in the way of the biological parents' relationship with their children or with each other.

To begin with, don't call the other parent "the ex." That puts the focus on the failed marriage rather than the fact that the person is still the child's parent. Always call the person by his or her name.

Some people are very good about not badmouthing the other parent in front of the children, but still there's tension in the air. Without you ever muttering a nasty word, the children can sense the strain and animosity between you and the other parent. Living with bad vibes between Dad and Stepdad or between Mom and Stepmom is harmful to emotional and physical health. To avoid tension in the air, you may need to take the "No badmouthing policy" one step further: Give a sincere compliment to the children about their parent, for example, "You have pretty eyes, just like your Mother." When their mother comes to pick up the kids, invite her in and say something like, "You have wonderful children, you've done a great job as a parent," and as they leave be sure to say, "I hope you all have a wonderful time together."

Don't get caught in the crossfire of post-divorce animosity by fanning the flames of mistrust. You'll have to learn how to be cordial, and if you're fighting, you'll have to learn how to stop and start cooperating. Try to understand what life is like from the other parent's perspective. Instead of assuming John is being "Disneyland Dad" while you get all the dirty work, understand the fact that his apartment is so small, it's more enjoyable to take the kids on outings. When you don't understand, ask for clarification instead of jumping to conclusions. Honor your agreements, focus on solutions that work for the kids, and respect each household's autonomy.

The greatest gift you can give to your spouse and stepchildren is showing them that even after a family splits up, you can all emerge as a supportive expanded family unit. You pave the way for this healing by treating the other parent with consideration and kindness and by saying something positive.

# ASK (NICELY) FOR APPRECIATION

Stepparenting may be a thankless task in terms of verbal appreciation from your stepkids, but that doesn't mean you don't deserve appreciation. The truth is your that loving care of your mate's children—whether it is on the daily level or only during vacations—is an incredible gift of love for which he or she should be grateful.

Unfortunately, many parents feel so guilty about the burden that their children place on their new mates that they don't want even to think about the gift you are giving, much less thank you for it. This can be especially true if you, the stepparent, do not have children yourself. After all, if both of you are asking similar things of one another, the guilt is lessened—you're both having to deal with a child ignoring you or throwing things at you. But if you are the only one making the loving sacrifice, then the burden of guilt can be heavy indeed on your spouse. Chances are he is not an ingrate, but so much in your debt that he wants to avoid the subject altogether. That's just human nature. If you owed someone $10,000 and couldn't pay it back right now, would you want to run into them every day? Probably you'd go out of your way to avoid them.

As a consequence, rather than wallow in resentment, you may have to ask specifically (and nicely!) for appreciation for all you do for his or her children. "This was a big deal with Harvey and me," said Lisa, "and we had many fights in which he would try to deny that I deserved appreciation. He would argue that it was good for me and therefore I shouldn't need thanks. Finally, one day we went to therapy and the therapist looked him in the eye and said, 'Being a full-time mother of someone else's kid is a big deal and you should just get it. Right now.' That did it. From that point on, Harvey went out of his way to say thanks and every Mother's Day he writes me a note saying how grateful he is for all the love I show to his son."

You do deserve a big pat on the back for your job as a step-parent. Besides giving yourself a hand on a regular basis, it's okay to ask your partner for some appreciation. If a note of thanks would ring your chimes, let him know. If you'd love a backrub to acknowledge all you've done this week for her son, let her know. When it comes to appreciation, it never hurts to ask.

# BE WILLING TO BE FLEXIBLE

Parenting children requires a great deal of give and take: "Can you chauffeur Tina to the soccer game so I can take Lucy to her swim meet?" "Julia is sick; which of us can stay home more easily?" With stepkids, there are even more logistical issues to be worked out, particularly if there is joint custody. The whos, whats, and wheres expand exponentially when there are two (or more!) households to consider, and "yours, mine, and our" kids to consider. The whole delicate balance can be thrown into a tailspin, unless you are all willing to be flexible.

Nowhere is this more true than in the emotionally charged issue of holiday planning. You've agreed to alternate having the kids on Christmas Day, and this year it's your turn—but her family is having the first reunion of all their relatives in twenty years and so she wants them this year again. Or it's her turn, and you've planned a romantic trip to Hawaii just for the two of you, and suddenly she's in the hospital and you have to cancel your plans and take the kids. Or he just doesn't show up to take the kids on Father's Day as promised.

These all can be hot-button issues, potential flashpoints between you and your spouse, between your spouse and the ex, between you and the kids, or any permutation thereof. It's easy when plans go awry, especially holiday plans, for the people involved to lose their tempers and get very rigid: "He always leaves us in the lurch." "We're always the ones doing the chauffeuring." "No way am I going to ruin my vacation to accommodate her!" While such feelings are natural and may even be appropriate, they don't do a lot for resolving the situation in a manner that maximizes the potential for happiness.

Flexibility—and an eye on what's most important—will help defuse most of these potential trouble spots. Why can't you celebrate Christmas on December 26? By doing it joyfully, you'll have a better time, and the kids won't have to live in a morass of hostility and anger.

"Fred's ex-wife refused to do her share of shuttling the kids back and forth," remembers Rosemary. "She claimed that since the divorce was his idea, we would have to do all of the driving, about ninety miles round-trip each Friday evening to pick up his daughter and each Sunday evening to bring her back. Of course it was grossly unfair. But Fred always said that seeing his daughter was more important than being right, and because I love him, I help out as much as I can." Flexibility is the ability to roll with the punches—and since step-parenting is full of punches, we should all limber up!

# ENCOURAGE A HEALTHY RELATIONSHIP WITH THE EX-SPOUSE

Maybe you and your mate get along just fine with your exes. If so, congratulations! That makes life much easier, not only for you but for your kids. But unfortunately, many of us harbor great anger or resentment toward the person we used to be married to, or the person who used to be married to our current spouse, and that can make life quite unpleasant, especially for the young ones.

When you choose to have children with someone, you are not only making a lifelong commitment to your children, but you also are creating a lifelong tie to their other parent, whether you choose to acknowledge it or not. When we hang on to anger and refuse to forgive our former spouse, or encourage our current spouse to be angry and bitter, we prevent the full creation of the loving family we desire now. As the Sufis say, "As long as there is room in your heart for one enemy, your heart isn't a safe place for a friend."

We can't control what our ex or our spouse's ex will do. But we can practice from a distance being openhearted toward them and blessing them on their journey. And because we may have less volatile feelings toward our mate's ex, we can also encourage him or her to forgive if necessary.

Such encouragement can reap beautiful rewards. We know a woman in her twenties, Louise, who was very resentful toward her stepmother of four years. She didn't like her and didn't intend to try. Then Louise got engaged and began to plan her wedding. One day her father, holding onto his anger over his divorce from Louise's mother more than ten years before, proclaimed that he would not contribute a cent to the wedding if Louise's mother were present. Louise was in despair, threatening to elope and angry that her parents couldn't come together in peace even for her wedding day. About a week later, she got a call from her father. He had changed his mind. "I know that my stepmother worked on him," Louise told us. Suddenly she saw her stepmother in a whole new light and their relationship has finally taken off.

Practice and encourage forgiveness—if only for the sake of the kids.

# NEGOTIATE RELATIONSHIPS WITH RELATIVES

One of the fall-outs from divorce is not just changed relationships between parents and kids, but between kids and their grandparents and other relatives. Depending on the situation, grandparents can suddenly find themselves out in the cold, unable to see or talk to their beloved grandchildren. This can send them into a panic and set them against you, the interloper whom they believe is standing in their way.

As a stepparent, you can do both your kids and their extended family a big favor by encouraging continuing relationships with the ex's relatives. "One of the consequences of being a stepmother that I never would have foreseen," says Nancy, "is a very strong relationship with Fred's ex–mother-in-law. She knows I am a good caretaker of her grandchildren and that I encourage her relationship with the kids, and she appreciates that. As a consequence, she would do almost anything for me."

Every kid needs as many people to love him, to nurture her, as possible, and we stepparents must not only acknowledge the truth of that, but we must also work with our spouses to make sure the extended family's bonds remain strong. This might mean anything from letting the kids go to Grandma Pat's on Easter rather than be with you, to creating occasions at your house where the steprelatives can come and see the kids.

Only you and your spouse know what is best for you and your kids. But don't let bad feelings stand in your way of encouraging as much connection as possible. Don't assume that the grandparents know that they are welcome. Tell them in a letter or in person that you want them to stay involved in the grandkids' lives. If they live out of town, follow through by sending pictures.

Kinship is a connection by blood, marriage, or adoption; it's a relationship among people who have an affinity for one another. Perhaps your stepson, Josh, is close friends with his cousin who is the nephew of your husband's former wife. The friendship between Josh and his cousin doesn't go away just because his parents are no longer married. Kinship is the branching out of the nuclear family. When you took on a stepfamily, whether you noticed it right off the bat or it took you a while to feel the impact, the fact is you've not only got next-of-kin, you've got widespread, far-reaching kinships.

Take pride in all your connections. Honor the depth and breadth of the entire family unit. You'll develop many surprising resources to call in a crisis, if you do.

# KEEP THE KIDS OUT
# OF THE MIDDLE

Most likely, the children under your care are in a difficult situation vis-à-vis their two sets of parents. They know, if only intuitively, if there is any tension between them, and often feel it is their responsibility to smooth the waters and create peace. But because the problem is an adult one and not of their making, they can never truly restore harmony, and therefore the children can end up feeling like failures.

Kids have a tendency to feel responsible for whatever goes wrong between the adults in their lives, but we can make their lives as painless as possible if we agree with our spouse to keep the kids out of the middle—out of the middle of any disagreement between the two of us, and out of the middle of any muddles between us and their other parent.

Patricia can't stand her ex-husband, so instead of dealing with him directly, she uses her fourteen-year-old daughter, Paige, as the go-between. Paige hates the position because her dad uses guilt and bribery to manipulate her into doing what he wants. Patricia is afraid of his temper, so has defaulted on her responsibility to protect her daughter from such conflicts. But as the adults, you must shield the children from the warfare.

This means, of course, remembering that "little pitchers have big ears" and to confine our grousing about the exes till the kids are truly out of earshot. And it means not using the child as a conduit between the two of us in a fight—"Tell your mother I am furious she bought the new dishwasher without consulting me," or "Tell your stepfather he is a stingy pig"—and, most important, not using the child as a messenger between our house and the ex's. No telling the kids to ask Dad for the support check or to ask Mom to change the pick-up arrangements for next week. If you need to change the arrangements, call her directly. If you're concerned about all the clothes you bought for little Emily that she took back to Dad's and you haven't seen since, call him and ask that the clothes be sent back next time.

We shouldn't ask the children to do our dirty work for us; after all, we are the adults here and so should shoulder the burden. Make a pact with your spouse to keep the kids out of the middle. The children will be better off for it.

# TALK ABOUT
# FINANCIAL CONCERNS

Money is a hot spot for any couple, and the realities of stepfamilies only make it more so. Child-support payments you or your spouse must make, ex-spouses' failures to pay child support, the myriad of items you, the stepparent, end up providing for your stepchildren—any or all of these can cause resentment or open warfare.

We once knew a couple, Grace and Charles, who broke up over his resentment concerning money. Grace had three kids from a former marriage and an ex who failed to make his child-support payments. In the beginning, Charles, who was childless, was willing to take up the slack. But over the years it got to him. "While Grace did work, her job did not cover the expenses of three kids. I was keeping the family together financially and not getting any credit for it, from either Grace or the kids. I was resentful and began having affairs as a way to exert my independence. I got tired of it being so lopsided financially—I even bought a house that we could all live in—and so when I met Louise, who had no children, I just took off. I'm sorry that I never was able to tell Grace how I felt, but every time I tried, she brushed me off."

Money issues are never easy to talk about, particularly if the truth is that you feel resentful about the situation with your spouse. It's hard to own up to such feelings—they may seem petty or selfish. But as Charles' story demonstrates, if you let the situation fester, it can cause an irreparable breach in your relationship. So first, ask yourself some hard questions: Is the financial situation you find yourself in fair? If not, who is carrying more of the burden? How do you and he or she truly feel about that? Does the situation call for some creative thinking?

We know a couple, a childless woman and a man with a son, who resolved the problem uniquely. "We each contribute the exact same amount to our household expenses," says Mary Ellen, "and keep the rest for ourselves. Then I don't worry about what Bob is spending on his son. He does what he wants with the rest of his money and so do I."

Finding creative solutions depends first on acknowledging that there might be inequities that are causing bad feelings. So be honest with yourself first and then with your spouse—don't let money come between you.

# SEEK HELP WHEN NECESSARY

As much as the two of you love one another, communicate about the difficult things, and try to remain flexible and lighthearted, you may encounter situations that require outside help. Please don't feel badly about needing help—as we have said before, this is hard. And sometimes an outside perspective or suggestion is just what makes the difference.

"We could not have survived the first couple years," recalls Anna, "without our therapist. Bill and I were completely oblivious to the issues that divorce and remarriage with kids would raise. Plus we still had issues within our relationship to work out. Week after week we discovered that we weren't alone in confronting these problems and learned the negotiating skills we needed to communicate well with one another."

The following symptoms are indications you could benefit from professional assistance: 1) You and your partner are frequently locked into bitter conflict and arguments. 2) You feel depressed and hopeless about your situation. 3) Family conflicts lead to physical threats or violence. 4) One child in your family has been identified as the "troublemaker." 5) One or both of you is using drugs or alcohol to cope. 6) A child is having problems in school or with peers. 7) You get little or no satisfaction from family life.

Don't get bound up in denial. Emotional distress is prolonged if you ignore it. Whether you choose individual therapy, couples or family counseling, pastoral advice, or a support group depends on your situation and temperament.

Sandra and Greg, married four years, came to counseling with Judy because stepson Jeff was flunking out of junior high. They argued incessantly about how to deal with him—Greg wanted to send Jeff to live with his biological father; Sandra felt Greg was shirking his commitment to her by wanting her son out of the picture. Initially they thought if counseling could "fix Jeff" their family life would improve. After an initial evaluation they designed a treatment approach that included a stepparenting support group, brief marriage counseling, extra tutoring for Jeff, and single nights out for each of them. They put in considerable effort to face their problems. In the support group, they learned conflict resolution skills and made friends with others in the same boat. In marriage counseling they learned more productive ways of communicating. Tutoring gave Jeff a boost to his self-esteem because his grades went up and took the parents out of the homework battles. Single nights out relieved the tension of never having time for reflecting or relaxing with friends.

Seeking outside help is not a sign of weakness but rather a sign of your loving intention to do all that you can to heal the wounds, right the wrongs, and be responsible parents and loving partners.

# MAKE TIME FOR
# THE TWO OF YOU

This is one of the unique challenges blended families present to us. When we fall in love and are childless, there is usually a period of time in which we get to be alone with our beloved, basking in our newfound love and learning about all of his or her idiosyncrasies. Moonlit walks, long dinners, uninterrupted hours for lovemaking ... all of the delicious togetherness that is the mortar that holds the bricks of our relationship together.

But with children on the scene, such togetherness—if it can be accomplished at all in the courtship phase with baby-sitters and the ex-spouse's visitation schedule—is usually short-lived. Soon there you are—all together and often none too happy about it. "That is one of the real challenges of our relationship," says Shirley, whose husband has three kids who live with them full-time. "Because Mick is a widower, we didn't have more than two minutes alone before I met the kids. I like them and we get along pretty well, but I still long for time for just the two of us. I mean, sometimes it seems as though the three of them are purposely trying never to give us a minute alone."

Unless you are a very occasional stepparent, you probably have feelings similar to Shirley's. Every couple needs time alone, but somehow when it is the other person's children who are standing in the way, it's easy to feel particularly resentful.

There are all kinds of ways to find the time, no matter what your financial circumstances. "Bill and I go out to dinner alone once a week," says Anna. "That's our special time." Stephanie and Don drop their kids off at Grandma's for the weekend four times a year and take off in their trailer. Stuart and Liz use the time when the kids are at their other parents' house to reconnect again.

It doesn't matter how you do it; what matters is that you take the time to do it. Remember—it was your love for this person that got you into the situation in the first place. Nurture that love and the rest will be easier.

# OFFER PRIVATE TIME TO
# KIDS AND THEIR PARENTS

When the Sanchez family came to counseling, they were eager to find better ways to live harmoniously together. It took only a few sessions to identify one of the fallacies they had been operating under. The parents thought that in order to make a successful adjustment as a blended household, they should no longer spend time alone with their biological kids. They worried that if they spent one-on-one time with their own kids, the others would be jealous and that would drive a wedge between them.

While talking this over, the Sanchezes discovered that this mistaken notion was actually creating more friction in their household. Maria missed the private outings and the mother-daughter talks that she and Anna had shared for the previous six years when they lived alone. José longed for boys' nights and camping weekends with his twins. With the best of intentions Maria and José had stopped all separate outings for fear the others might feel left out. They admitted to missing their private time with their own kids. It turns out that the kids also longed for alone time with their biological parents. When the Sanchezes reinstated the outings and allowed for private moments, they all felt the sadness disappearing. By hanging out as they had done before they were a blended family, everyone felt less of a sense of loss and more energy when they were all together.

Becoming a stepfamily is a wonderful event, but it's also accompanied by loss. The loss of privacy, the loss of a previous way of life, the loss of routine, and the loss of the familiar. Perhaps it also means loss of friends because of a move to a new neighborhood or new city. You'll lessen the loss when you allow for private time between parent and child. Just as you need time alone with your spouse to keep your relationship thriving, the kids need time to fortify the love and communication with their parent.

Be sensitive to the need for private talks and one-on-one outings. No matter how much you like the stepchildren, or they like you, they still need time alone with your spouse. "Sometimes just a smidgen of privacy with their mom makes a big difference in the way the kids are treating me," says Hank. "I don't mind when my stepdaughter Brynn goes out to dinner alone with her dad," says Rene. "It's a treat for both of them and, besides it gives me some much-needed solitude."

Try not to feel threatened by your stepchild's need for personal moments with his or her parent. Offer to give them privacy by saying, "I can see you'd like to talk in private." Make yourself scarce. Tell them it's okay with you so that they don't feel guilty. Your stepkids and partner will appreciate your mature generosity, and you can have a quiet house all to yourself.

# WALK A MILE IN YOUR SPOUSE'S SHOES

Empathy is the capacity to feel the reality of another person's situation, even though it is different from yours. It is an expansion of the heart, an act of love that says even though I'm over here in my circumstance, I am aware of and concerned for you over there in your circumstance.

For us stepparents, empathy helps us stay connected to our spouse through the various ups and downs that the children in our lives will create. It helps us remember that while it is hard for us that little Jillian won't speak to us, it is also hard for her father, our beloved. How must it feel when your own flesh and blood tells your wife, whom you love deeply, that she hates her? How must it feel when the son you care for so much refuses to sit down at the same table with your husband? We of course feel badly if these things happen, but our spouse, whose child is acting so badly, must feel terrible too. "It hurts deeply to see my son and husband fighting. I can't even explain the agony of seeing the two most precious people in my life calling each other names and refusing to cooperate," Helena told her stepparenting group.

If you're having difficulty empathizing with your spouse's position, try this simple exercise. Take a five-minute break, sit in a quiet corner, close your eyes, and bring your partner into focus. Think about their day and all that they are doing. Look at their face and imagine what life is like from their perspective. What is it like to entrust the care of your child to another person? What is it like when their child is unhappy? In group, Wayne, along with other stepparents, came to a new awareness of Helena's pain when he did this exercise. As the stepparents began to view home life from their spouses' perspective, they understood that the biological parent often feels on the verge of another disastrous failure when there are hurtful encounters between their beloved spouse and precious child. They feel sad, helpless, and deeply troubled.

When we remember his or her pain, rather than just focusing on our own, we allow our hearts to open in love toward our spouse. Rather than seeing them as the enemy who got us into the horrid situation in the first place, we are able to see them as fellow travelers on this particular journey. Like us, he is trying the best he knows how; she is doing the best she can. When we walk a mile in our beloved's shoes we can be truly grateful for the priceless treasure of the child we are sharing.

# LOOK FOR THE BLESSINGS

To thrive as a stepparent requires courage, character, and commitment for sure, but it also calls you to count your blessings, see the positive, and look for the silver linings. The positive side of human nature is a mighty force, and when you cultivate its potential you can turn the gloomiest situation bright. The folks who succeed in the stepparenting department do so in large part because of their ability to see the positive and to be grateful for the tiniest of blessings.

Maintaining a positive, upbeat attitude is a core ingredient in winning in any situation. If you believe that your living situation is "awful" you will probably create unhappy interactions. Likewise if you channel your inner thoughts and spoken words to encouraging ideas and uplifting suggestions, your life will take on a positive aura. When you get up in the morning and believe that today is going to be a great day with your stepkids and spouse, and that tomorrow will be even greater, you see to it that it happens.

Think back to when you met and dated your spouse. What drew you to him or her in the first place? When you met the children, what were the warm feelings you had? Now write down five blessings that these souls have brought into your life. Describe the joy and excitement that's been added to your life because of them.

Be specific about the blessings you're receiving. Say them out loud at the dinner table, whisper them in your sweetheart's ear, leave a note pasted to the bathroom mirror for everyone to read. List the blessings in your journal each night for one month. If you know you have to write them down, you'll get into the habit of looking for the joy.

Keep your eyes open for the tiniest windfalls. "On Father's Day we gave Will a list of the many blessings we received from having him in our life," recall Judy and Amanda. "We wrote down that he taught us to appreciate the Beatles and Mozart, how to cook veggie burgers, and the advantages of eating with chopsticks." Be sure to tell your sweetheart often how much they've enriched your lives.

"As soon as Matt and I got home, we began recounting the horrors and imagined mistreatment of our day, until that was all we were seeing," said Christine. "Then while watching *Oprah*, I learned about keeping a grateful journal, which changed the way I view my blended family. Each day I list three things I'm grateful for—watching Jake read a bedtime story to my daughter, seeing the love on his face when his son calls, listening as he teaches our son to play the guitar."

By dwelling on the unhappy incidents of yesterday, you end up wallowing in pain and apprehension missing the pleasure of the moment. In this moment, right now, can you see the beauty and the blessings surrounding you and your spouse?

# INTERACTING
# WITH THE KIDS

*We learn to do something by doing it.*
*There is no other way.*

—John Holt

# ASSUME THE BEST

Even though four-year-old Amanda didn't see her father regularly, she wasn't about to accept Will as a stand-in. In fact, the first time she met him she opened the front door, kicked him as hard as she could, and loudly warned, "Leave my mother alone." Fortunately, he was good-natured and understanding about it; he rather admired her spunk. "Even though I was mortified," remembers Judy, "he remained positive, appreciating her directness and spirit. In the ensuing years, no matter how she ignored him, scowled at him, or frowned, he always assumed the best about her. Eventually she saw him as her ally."

Children of divorce suffer setbacks to self-esteem and their sense of security is shaken. Often plagued by guilt and shame, they feel responsible for their parents' divorce. They've lost a portion of childhood innocence and are forced to deal with adult issues before they have appropriate skills for the task. They worry that something else might go wrong, and they may feel pessimistic. These anxieties and worries are frequently acted out in troublesome behaviors. If you recognize the depth of the despair children can feel when biological parents no longer live together, you won't misinterpret your stepchild's sullenness, orneryness, or belligerence as character flaws, and you won't take it personally.

Bad behavior is frequently evidence of fear, confusion, frustration, and insecurity. If you view your stepson as a "little creep" who is trying to make your life miserable, you'll set a pessimistic tone for your entire relationship. When you assume the worse, you put a negative spin on a perfectly normal emotional process, unpleasant behavior is magnified, and your relationship becomes bogged down in misunderstanding.

You can assist your stepchild in resolving his upset by assuming the best. "It's confusing to have a stepfather" is better than "Don't ignore me when I talk to you." If you point out his cranky disposition, he'll get stuck believing that's all there is about him, and things will rapidly slide downhill. The worse your stepchild is behaving, the more he needs your kindness, recognition, and genuine appreciation. By assuming the best, the best can blossom.

Believe that your problem is solvable, expect good things to come, and don't put energy into figuring out who is right or who is wrong. How you view the child will make a difference, because when you assume the best you create an environment in which children feel safe and respected. In such an environment defensive behaviors melt, and your stepchildren are able to open their hearts and let you in.

# ALLOW THEM TO EXPRESS
# HOW THEY FEEL

Feelings are incredibly powerful. In his book *Emotional Intelligence,* Daniel Goleman describes research that shows that most of our reactions to things—our likes and dislikes, our fears and angers—are controlled by the most primitive part of our brains, which operate in an instinctive way to protect us. The most advanced part of the brain, the neocortex, is engaged only if we pause between feeling and reaction to think about the various consequences of acting on our feelings. Unless we do pause, we are responding instinctively, based on patterns that were laid down in the earliest years of childhood. That's why one of the components of emotional intelligence, says Goleman, is an ability to identify our feelings and have some choice in how and when we express them.

As caretakers of children, it is one of our sacred duties to develop emotional intelligence in ourselves and pass those skills along. Nowhere is this more valuable than in helping our children deal with the strong feelings being part of a blended family can create. First, we can teach children to recognize their feelings—"I'm mad; I'm sad; I'm glad"—and then begin to see that feelings are just energy in motion that we can choose to do something about or not.

One process that might help your family situation is the use of a talking stick. This is an American Indian tradition in which people sit in a circle. When a person feels moved to speak, she holds the "talking stick." While she is holding the stick, she has the floor and no one can interrupt or rebut what she is saying. The rest of the circle must listen in silence. When she is done, someone else can take up the stick, but he too must speak from the heart. Again no one can rebut, deny, disagree with, or counter anyone else's truth. Rather it is up to the listeners to simply receive what the speaker is saying.

This is a great way for kids to get their feelings out about a situation they find themselves in and for them to begin to understand that their feelings are just that—feelings. If you do it often enough, they will begin to see that their feelings change—hate one day might be mild dislike another; love might be there one day and not the next. As they begin to see their feelings as a river on which they can witness themselves, a flow on which their consciousness rests but is somehow separate from, they can begin to ride the currents of feelings more graciously. And as they see that you are able to receive their feelings, no matter how "horrible," without being destroyed, they will begin to use their feelings less as weapons and more as vehicles for connection.

# DO A PHYSICAL
# ACTIVITY TOGETHER

As a stepparent you'll often feel as if you're in the middle of a nightmare in which you're the last person chosen to play on the team. The trick for feeling better is to find ways to have fun together even when you're not sure anyone wants you there in the first place. Physical activity—games, horsing around, and goofing off—are the quickest, most productive ways to bond as a expanded family.

Perhaps you've gotten so caught up in the day-to-day grind of keeping your blended household operating that you've forgotten about having a good time. Often stepparents want so much to be accepted that they're hypersensitive to rejection. In fact they become oversensitive, seeing rejection in every action. If you recognize this tendency in yourself, the best way to overcome it to discover each other through free, noncompetitive, lighthearted, robust play. Add a daily dose of silliness, dancing, singing, and smiling to your routine. By placing your emphasis on having fun rather than making your life together ideal, you can avoid many wicked stepparent pitfalls.

Everyone wins when you're having fun. Doing physical activities once a week is a good way to ignite the joy that holds a family together. A hardy workout lets off steam and melts anger in nonhurtful ways. You can soothe rivalries and resentments through a game of tennis, baseball, tag, or by playing hide-and-seek. Climb trees, walk in the rain and splash in puddles, go for a hike, take square dancing lessons, go bicycling, try rollerblading. Get out of the house and jump around. It's vital to your emerging family to communicate about the nitty-gritty and nuances of combining your lives, but remember that communication is frequently best when it's unspoken. You don't have to talk endlessly about all the problems; sometimes it's better to keep your frustrations to yourself and work it out by playing hard.

Try dividing up the teams so that each child gets to be on a team once with their own parent and once with the stepparent. Try having siblings together first, and then try mix-matched sets. You burn off excess energy and resolve unspoken conflicts with a friendly water fight.

Put on the boogie-woogie music and prance around before dinner. Sing a song while peeling the potatoes, turn off the television, and get the music blaring. Soon everyone will be tapping their toes, and you'll all forget at least for a moment that you're not blood-related. It's impossible to be sour when you're playing volleyball, laughing, whistling, and horsing around.

# ACKNOWLEDGE THE TRUTH
# OF THEIR SITUATION

The truth is incredibly powerful, and we should never underestimate its value in dealing with kids. So often adults have a tendency to sugarcoat things when talking to kids, to "put the best face on it," to evade or even downright lie. But kids are truth-seeking missiles—the more we tell the truth, and even more important, acknowledge the truth of their situation, the more they will respect us and treat us well in return.

This means saying, "Yes, I understand that you don't want to be here. It must be hard to have to shuffle between houses just because a judge said so" when a child complains about the arrangements, rather than, "Now come on, it will be fun," or, "You don't mean that," or even worse, "That makes me feel bad." (It's your job as the adult to take care of them, not to ask them to take care of you and your feelings.) Let's face it—they are in a tough situation. Would you like to have to live in two places and move back and forth on alternate weeks? Or up and go to another house every fourth weekend?

Kids need their feelings validated, not ignored, denied, or overrun by your feelings, and children in stepfamilies have some pretty tough feelings to deal with. The truth is they didn't ask to be in your life any more than you asked them to be in yours, and the fact that they are can create strong feelings of anger, jealousy, or even guilt. As step-parents, we need to validate the truth of how they feel.

"My proudest moment as a stepparent," remembers Anna, "came when Zoe was about twelve. Her brother was living with us full-time by then, but she was still with her mother and visiting us every other weekend. We were having a pleasant dinner and I had just made some innocuous comment. She turned and said, 'Why don't you go away and never come back.' I was terribly hurt and shocked. She and I had always had a wonderful, close relationship for over ten years. This seemed to come out of the blue. I remained quiet and let a couple of hours pass so I could think about the situation. Suddenly it came to me. She was jealous of the fact that her brother was living with us full-time and guilty over not wanting to be with her mother. If I disappeared, she wouldn't be having such feelings. I went up to her room, took her into my arms and very quietly said, 'I think some-times you wish you were my little girl and could live here all the time.' She burst into tears, and we hugged for a long time. Nothing else was said, but we never had another difficult moment."

Sometimes acknowledging the truth of the situation is very sim-ple: "Yes I see you are very angry." Other times, as Anna's story demonstrates, it requires going below the surface to touch the deeper truth. Either way, our commitment to the truth will help guide us moment to moment.

# BE PREPARED FOR
# THE COLD SHOULDER

If you are new at this, you might be surprised if you get a less than totally enthusiastic response from your stepkids. After all, they're great, as their parent, your spouse, has told you, and you know you're great, so what's the problem? The problem, of course, is that they may have very complex feelings that you have no awareness of about the situation: Stacey has enjoyed being the "woman" in Daddy's life for several years and now you've come along to replace her; Tim has feelings of hostility toward all women because of his relationship with his mother, and you are now a convenient target; you are being blamed for the divorce by your wife's ex who is teaching the kids actively to hate you. Any number of things could be—and are—going on.

At the very least, the kids are wary—Is this man going to try to replace my father? Is she going to treat me fairly or will she show favoritism to her own kids? Will I get time with my father or will he be so absorbed by her that he will ignore me? None of this is a recipe for instant intimacy, and you shouldn't expect it. Until they've figured out where they stand, and have gotten to know and trust you at least a bit, be prepared for the cold shoulder. This could range anywhere from a certain cool, polite formality—"Yes, Mrs. Cleaver, I do like math," to favoritism—Kim holds Daddy's hand crossing the street, but won't take yours—all the way to downright hostility: "I hate you and wish you'd drop dead."

So many of us enter stepparenting expecting the best—and that's good, a positive attitude is important—that we get thrown completely by the cold shoulder, fearing that it will go on forever. Chances are it won't—especially if you don't take it too seriously and continue to be your kind, funny, down-to-earth self. If we get on our high horse—I'm your stepmother now and you *must* love me—or if we try and force intimacy before they are ready—It's *so* wonderful that we can be together, kiss, kiss—the cold shoulder will escalate or harden into a perpetual stance.

In a way, being a stepparent is a little like wooing someone who's reluctant to get into a relationship. Too much intimacy or too many demands and they will get scared off. Just the right touch of friendliness and care, a bit of mystery and humor, and they will come running to your side. Well, eventually, anyway.

# GIVE THEM TIME

This is a corollary to "Be prepared for the Cold Shoulder." Everyone needs time to develop positive feelings toward other people, and just because you have become (or are about to become) these children's stepparent doesn't mean they will love you right away. They need time to adjust to the reality of the new situation and to understand their place in it. With time they will see that you are fair and on their side. With time, they will see that you are great at games, or a good listener, or just the person to help them with their writing assignments. In other words, with time, they will see you more and more for who you really are, rather than merely a blank screen for their fear and anger.

This doesn't mean you will necessarily have the kind of close relationship that you might truly want, but that you will both be able to accept one another and live in basic harmony. "Michael was cold to me for the first couple years of my being in his life," says Anna. "But as time went on, he grew to accept, and, I think, even love me in his own way. I was the one to turn to for homework help, the one who was always there if he needed something. We were never as close as Zoe and I have been, but we were able to live peaceably with one another. Several times he made me birthday or Mother's Day cards in which he expressed strong feelings that he was uncomfortable verbalizing. I used to feel bad about it, but after talking to lots of parents of boys, ultimately, I don't think it is any different than many mother-son relationships."

As Anna's story demonstrates, relating to our stepchildren is a lot like relating to our relatives. Some we may feel incredibly close to; toward others we feel a warmth; still others are a challenge to connect with. Somehow, with time, we learn to accept them all, relishing the deep closeness we feel toward some and appreciating the good parts of those who are a challenge to us.

By giving our stepchildren time to grow to like and love us, by not panicking if the warm feelings don't flow immediately, we give them the psychological space they need to make us part of their family. Maybe we'll end up as a cherished parent, or perhaps be thought of more like an eccentric, but beloved aunt. But as we continue in their lives, we will end up being accepted as "part of the family."

# TEACH RESPECT

While you're acknowledging the truth of the situation, expecting the cold shoulder, and giving them time, this doesn't mean that you have to put up with maltreatment. Your stepkids don't have to love you or even like you, but you do have the right to ask for the kind of respect any other human being would receive. You may have to teach them how to give it to you.

Teaching respect begins with an internalized attitude—it says, "I know that I will not allow myself to be walked all over as doormat, but neither am I so afraid that I *am* a doormat that I see disrespect in every little action." Rather it is a quiet self-assuredness that requests that you be treated well.

This can be tricky territory, because it's easy in the heat of the moment to feel disrespect from a hostile stepchild and to find yourself in a pitched battle over being treated well. The trick is not to let it become an adversarial situation, but through your (and your spouse's) modeling of respect for one another and the children, you set the example for how you want to be treated.

Sometimes this doesn't work, and you find yourself in a direct confrontation. You and Tommy are alone and you have just asked him to pick up his toys and he has replied, "You're not my mother, I don't have to listen to you." Probably, you and your spouse have come to an agreement already about this—for example, Tommy must pick up his toys before dinner when he is in our house—as well as agreed upon a strategy for noncompliance—no dessert, say. So what do you do?

What *not* to do is to start yelling back about how you deserve respect as his stepmother. Instead, if you acknowledge the truth of the situation and in your firm, yet calm control, things should go pretty well: "You're right, I'm not your mother, and I can't make you pick up your toys, but right now you are here. One of our house rules, as you know, is that you pick up your toys before dinner. If you don't you won't get dessert. It's your choice."

Teaching respect can range from refusing to answer unless addressed in a civil manner (which you announce in a very neutral voice) to saying something like "Ouch" when a stepchild makes a hurtful comment. Exactly what to do when is something you need to feel your way through. You don't have to stand for abuse—but don't make a federal case over it. Again, lightheartedness is your ally.

# RESPECT THEIR LIKES
# AND DISLIKES

To earn respect from our stepchildren, we must show it to them in return. This can be difficult when they are being mean to you. One simple way to establish a sense of respect is to discover their likes and dislikes and then try to honor them when the stepchildren are with you.

Jason doesn't like eggs? Rather than ridiculing that or trying to get him to broaden his culinary horizons, offer pancakes with a remark such as, "I know you don't like eggs, so I've made pancakes just for you." Jennifer hates pink, your favorite color. Offer to go to the hardware store with her to find a color for her room that she will enjoy.

It should go without saying that we try to please those we live with by indulging their little idiosyncracies, but somehow, as a stepparent, the likes and dislikes of our stepchildren can be annoying. Perhaps it is because we don't have a long history with these children yet; we weren't there when little Mark caught his first fish on a trip with Dad and now is a fishing fanatic. It just seems like a boring waste of time to us. We weren't present when baby Megan first took her stuffed bunny to bed at six months; all we know now, eight years later, is that the thing is torn and smells and "she's too old" for such a thing.

When we respect our stepkids' likes and dislikes, when we go out of our way to plan the fishing trip, serve food without onions, or let him sleep with the fan on in the winter because the noise is soothing, we demonstrate our care. We show them that we see who they are and that who they are matters to us. We also show that this arrangement is not just a one-way street. They may have to come to our house and live by our *policies*, but we are willing to change and adapt for them too. We're willing to give up chicken on the bone, the chance to sleep late on weekends, an orderly guest room, because the stepkids are important to us.

Parents make such accommodations all the time and kids don't generally even consciously notice. We stepparents are coming in later in the game and have to play catch-up. It's okay to point the adaptations you've made out—as long as you do it in a loving, non-guilt trip way. These gestures go a long way toward demonstrating our concern for their happiness and well-being. What little thing can you do to make your stepchild feel loved today?

# DO IT THEIR WAY WHEN YOU CAN

Children cooperate more easily and behave more responsibly when given a choice in the matters that affect them, such as visitation, phone calls, and scheduled activities. Involving children in age-appropriate decision-making gives them a feeling of security, a sense of belonging, and helps them feel less a helpless casualty of divorce and more in control of their lives.

Residential custody with one parent is best for children under the age of five. They need the routine that a primary caretaker provides. As children grow, they can adjust to spending more time with the noncustodial parents, but they still need to be informed about when visits will occur, what activities are planned, and what the schedule might be. Older children deserve to have input into changes the parents are considering. School-age kids have friends, school activities, and social schedules that need to be taken into consideration. Teens may express a desire to move and live with another parent. Such wishes call for your thoughtful examination without making the child feel guilty or disloyal.

When fifteen-year-old Kristie, who lived with her mother and stepfather from age four, decided she wanted to go live with her father, her mother was shaken initially, but her stepfather recognized the courage it took for her to voice her desire. He understood that her need to live with her dad was sincere, and he empathized with her emotional struggle to keep everyone satisfied. He helped her sort through the pros and cons and negotiate a workable solution.

In the blending of households, and the juggling of visitation, kids often feel they have no rights. In some ways this is true, because the adults are making so many decisions on behalf of the child. To minimize their feelings of helplessness, give them as much control as you can over the little things.

For example, Will wanted to attend Amanda's fourth-grade concert, but Amanda wasn't thrilled about having him there. "If you'd rather go with just your mother, that's okay with me," he said. After thinking it over, she said he could come on one condition—"that you wear your suit." Will seldom wore a suit but for that occasion, he willingly obliged her.

His willingness to do it her way set the tone for the give-and-take required when families blend. When possible, he would do things the way she preferred—drive down her "favorite street" on the way to school, or let her choose the music in the car. He told her, "I do things for you because you do things for me. You turn your music down when it gets too loud and you get off the phone when I need to make a call." He was careful to acknowledge all she did for him. And likewise when possible, he would honor her requests and preferences.

# USE YOUR INTUITION

You've probably already figured out that despite all the books claiming to tell you what to do, all the childrearing theories, there are no rules in parenting—or in stepparenting. It all depends on the situation and the people involved. That's why some of our suggestions are followed by their opposites—often both are true, sometimes even at the same time!

Recognizing the truth of this can be nerve-wracking, because we want to do the right thing and wish there were hard and fast rules that we could just learn and follow. But the truth is that every soul is different, and what he or she needs may be different from what anyone else needs, and may also be different moment by moment, day by day. That's what makes parenting so fascinating—you can't just figure it out once and for all. One day she needs slack, the next day a tight rein. One time he needs you to hold the line; another time he needs you to look the other way. Debbie responds to your care and attention by blossoming like a flower; Tina withers you with a glance if you try the same approach on her.

So what's a (step)parent to do? Besides getting good advice, we believe that you can only ever do two things: really get to know who this person is; and then follow your intuition. The more you understand the children under your care—*really* understand, not create stories that get in the way of understanding—the more you can read the signals moment to moment as they come up and follow what your heart tells you to do: now I should ask the delicate question; now I should keep my mouth shut; now I should request some time alone; now I should be there for him.

Unless you are tuned in to your stepchildren, you will be traveling blind, destined to make many wrong turns. But once you do tune in, you will be amazed what your intuition will begin to show you: Tom is angry and he thinks he's mad at me. If I go give him a hug, he'll feel better and the whole problem will blow over; Samantha needs someone to talk to, she's worried about something she can't tell her parents. Here's where I can finally be of help.

Following your intuition means staying openhearted toward your stepkids, no matter how they are behaving, for the information won't flow well if you are closed off to them. If you can remember you are in their lives in service to their souls, you will always be able to find your way back to them, no matter what is going on. From there, your heart will tell you what to do.

# FIND A WAY TO CONNECT

"When I was feeling particularly estranged from Michael," remembers Anna, "a friend of mine asked me what he was really interested in. 'Physics,' I replied. 'He really wants to be the next Albert Einstein.' 'So,' she said, 'if I were you, I'd learn all I could about physics—or at least Einstein. That way you will be able to meet him in an area of *his* interest.'

"What great advice. It was true that we had virtually no mutual interests. He loved baseball; I hated it. He loved science fiction; I hated it. I loved hot tubs and swimming and he was uncomfortable in water. No wonder we weren't connected—we had nothing in common! Now physics was also something I had less than zero interest in, but I did want to improve our relationship and I was fascinated by the person of Albert Einstein. So I got a biography and began to talk to him about it."

All healthy relationships have what therapist Daphne Rose Kingma calls the medium of connection—something that brings you together and keeps you together in the rough spots of a relationship. It can be anything—fishing, shopping, talking about feelings, gardening, windsurfing, taking long walks, reading books and talking about them—or lots of things. But whatever it is, it is something you both love doing—and love doing together.

In fact, when we choose our partner, we are partly choosing him or her based on the connection we feel when we do certain things together—sailing, fixing houses, visiting art museums, traveling. Likewise, when we are searching for a way to connect to our stepchildren, we need look no further than the things we both like to do—skiing, playing video games, biking—and find more occasions to do them together.

Perhaps, like Anna and Michael, you realize there is no natural medium of connection between you and your stepchild. Then do a bit of thinking about which of his or her hobbies or interests you might genuinely enjoy learning about. The connection you create through this simple act will go a long way toward making your relationship stronger—and more fun.

# MAKE YOUR HOUSE
# THEIR HOME

No matter what the living arrangements are for your stepkids, at least some of the time they are living in your house. Help them feel as though it is their home too. Whether it is allowing them to decorate their rooms exactly how they want them, helping them find a private corner somewhere that can be all their own if they can't have a room of their own, or displaying photos, school drawings, or Father's Day presents, you want them to feel that this is one of the places on Earth that's "theirs," even if they aren't there all the time. It will go a long way toward making them feel wanted, a part of the family even when they are away.

Try to be sensitive to all the ways they could feel their space is violated. "One time, Bill's kids came for winter vacation. They had been at their mother's for two months straight. Their room doubled as our guest room and we had had guests. They arrived late at night and went straight to bed. The first thing in the morning, the two of them, age three and six, came solemn-faced into our bedroom. 'We have to talk to you about something,' they declared. 'Someone has been playing with our toys!' Even though two months had passed, they recognized that everything wasn't exactly as they left it and were upset."

It may not be possible for your stepchildren to have their own room, but you can think of creative ways for them to feel comfortable in your house. One child we know who lives half-time with Mom and half-time with Dad always travels with his tent, which they set up at whichever house he is in. That tent is what gives him a sense of home. Other kids always travel with special pillows or dolls or stuffed animals. The point is to make them comfortable.

Even if their room has to double as a guest room, let them be the ones to create the decorating scheme. (You can always explain to adult visitors if you are uncomfortable.) Again, it will create a sense of ownership that will help transform "your" house into "our" house. The more pleasant you make being with you, the more they will enjoy being there. And the more you will enjoy yourself too.

# PUT OUT THE WELCOME MAT

Your stepkids don't know if they're welcome in your home and in your life unless you tell them so. In their minds, the only person you're really interested in is their dad or their mom. Kids often feel like excess baggage because they sense that you're only trying to get along with them for the sake of peace in the household or to win the good graces of their parent. In their minds those reasons aren't good enough for them to make an effort to get along with you, let alone appreciate your positive attributes. To do that they'll need a bigger purpose, a personal incentive.

They need to know that not only are they welcome in the house but that you're welcoming them into your life. The only way they'll come to believe this is if you demonstrate your delight over and over again by telling them in a thousand and one ways how glad you are to have them around.

Welcoming a child into your life begins by simply putting a smile on your face, by being cheerful and good-natured. When you come together after they've been staying with the other parent say, "Hi, honey, glad to see you." Tell them, "I miss you when you're away." Ask them, "Will you sit down with me and visit for a minute?" Even if they don't sit with you right away, by asking, you're letting them know that you're interested. They'll see the efforts you're making.

Tell them, "I hope you had a good time at your mom's." Even if they don't respond outwardly, inwardly they'll feel thankful that you aren't competing with the other parent.

Be proud of your stepchildren by displaying their pictures around the house. Be sure to hang their artwork. Ask about their day, notice when they're feeling blue, ask how you can help, invite their friends for dinner. Show interest in their lives.

The transition from one house to the other is not always smooth. Think about what it's like when you have to pack your bags and stay somewhere else for a weekend. It takes time to get back into the groove. These transitions require special patience on your part, so don't expect that the kids can bounce from one house to another without adjustment time.

Don't ignore them even if they're ignoring you. Greet them warmly even if you don't feel it. No need to be gloomy just because the kids are suspicious of you. Wouldn't you be too, if a stranger was sleeping with your daddy or mommy? Why should they trust you? Don't push yourself on them.

Your stepchild needs lots positive attention from you. When you drop what you're doing they'll feel your genuine interest. If you're sidetracked and can't be bothered they'll get the message that you just don't care.

# CREATE SPECIAL
# TRADITIONS AND RITUALS

Part of what makes a family a family is special traditions—"We always have ham on Easter." "We always open our birthday presents *after* dinner." "We always go camping over the Fourth of July weekend." Part of what is lost when families break up is precisely these special little rituals that bring so much pleasure, especially to kids.

Now that you have a new family, it is time to create some rituals of your own. It's likely, particularly if the kids are older, that if you try to recreate traditions that they used to do, it will stir up too many old, painful memories. (But ask—maybe they would love to go caroling again the Sunday before Christmas.) You'll probably be better off with rituals that are unique to your new family, particularly since the kids are shuffling between parents over the major holidays. An annual Halloween party for all their friends, a special birthday dinner at a restaurant alone with you and your spouse, a sleepover with the four of you in the back yard every summer solstice—the possibilities are endless.

When establishing such traditions, remember to have patience. It isn't a tradition the first time around. You've got to do the same thing a few times at the proscribed occasion before the pattern is set and the true enjoyment sets in—which at least partially comes from remembering all the other times you've done this and sharing those stories together: Remember the time when we were in the tent and the dog was barking and Dad went outside in the dark and slipped on the dog poop and landed on his butt? Remember the time John ate all of Stephanie's birthday cake? Remember when Alice forgot to hard-boil the Easter Eggs and they broke all over the lawn?

Take care to include everyone in the family (although don't get too bogged down by party-poopers—they most likely will come around if you be sure to include some things you know they enjoy, like swimming or chocolate fudge) in the creation of the event: Tom, you be in charge of games because you're so good at that; Mom will handle the barbecue; Dan, you do the signs for the doors.

The more special times you create, the more love and laughter will invade your family—whatever its configuration.

# PAUSE BEFORE RESPONDING

This one could also be called "Duck When Emotional Shrapnel Comes Your Way." You know what we're talking about—those purposely mean little comments your stepkids lob your way just to get a rise out of you: My mother knows how to do laundry better than you (honest, this really happened); I hate your cooking; you are mean and ugly. The purpose of such remarks is to wound, to hurt you as much as they feel they have been hurt.

If you match them and react out of anger or fear, you are only escalating the cycle of pain. Rather, if you pause before responding, if you duck and let the emotional shrapnel fly over your shoulder, you will be in a place to ask the question: Why is this being said now?

The answer to that question might surprise you. You might figure out that Autumn and you have been getting along great recently, and she's feeling disloyal to her mother and seeking to put some distance between you. You might discover that Jason is flunking out of school and seeking to divert attention away from that fact. You might realize that you have been favoring your daughter over Julia in subtle ways, and she has a right to be upset. You might decide the best thing to do is ignore such a remark, teach Hollis how to cook for himself, or learn how to do laundry better.

But you will never figure out what's going on or come up with the best solution if you react instinctively to such baiting. No one can.

In certain elementary schools around the country, kids are learning impulse control using a traffic light as a metaphor. When someone hurts you, they are taught, the red light goes on. You stop, acknowledge how you feel to yourself—That hurts, I'm mad. Then the yellow light goes on. You think about all the ways you can respond—punch the person, call him names, walk away, tell him how you feel—and what the likely outcome of each of those will be. Then, green light, you choose the best option.

Seems to us that that's a useful formula for all of us any time we find ourselves in a heated situation.

# BE SENSITIVE TO
# EMOTIONAL BLACKMAIL

Your stepchildren have one great weapon to use against you—you are not their parent. And they will use it both in true anguish as well as to manipulate the situation to get what they want. Your job is to be able to differentiate between manipulation and a real problem, between blackmail and their honest feelings. While it can be difficult, this is not impossible. Again, it takes knowing the heart of the child and listening to your intuition.

"Michael was about four and was with us for the weekend," says Anna. "We had just gone to get donuts for breakfast and he had two. Well, he wanted another and we said no. So he proceeded to pitch a fit in the car, saying that he wanted to go back to his mother's because we were so mean. I knew that he loved being with his father and I knew this was just to test us, to see if we would give in and let him have a third donut. So I turned around in the seat to face him and said, 'The next time you say that you better really mean it because if you do, we will take you back to your mother's.' Not only did that stop him in his tracks then, but he never pulled that trick on us again."

Sometimes emotional blackmail needs to be ignored, sometimes it should be confronted head-on. If you pause before you react and consult your higher wisdom, you will be able to figure out what to do. But remember—not everything is emotional blackmail. Don't dismiss true cries as extortion. Context is everything.

"The times that Michael really cried for his mother were very different," recalls Anna. "I remember one in particular. His father was working and it was late at night and I heard sobs coming from Michael's room. He was about ten and had just begun living with us full-time. I went in and sat next to him and asked what was wrong. He said, 'I miss my mother. No matter where I am, I am always missing someone.' His plight touched my heart. As a person who grew up in an intact family, I never had to experience that longing for the missing parent no matter where you are. I held him for a long time, while he cried over the truth of his situation."

# STAY OUT OF SIBLING RIVALRY
## AS MUCH AS POSSIBLE

Kay has raised six children—two siblings from her first marriage, two stepchildren, and two children from her present marriage. Here's the bad news: "The kids fought a lot, picked on each other, and generally caused us misery," said Kay. But here's the good news: "The stepbrothers, who were the meanest to each other, have in their late twenties become the closest of friends," reports Kay. "We just wished they would have spared us the grief and gotten along when they were living at home," adds Kent. But there's more good and bad news: "Now that the kids are grown, they're close and they love to get together for family reunions at our house," says Kay. "Yup, they bring the nine grandkids, stay too long, and won't go home," teases Kent.

The most productive approach to sibling rivalry is: number one, stay calm; and number two, get their attention using humor. Nagging, begging, threatening, getting in the middle, or being the judge are techniques you've probably tried so many times that the kids mostly ignore you. The standard "You must be nice to your brother" is not an effective tool for soothing sibling rivalry. They've heard it before; besides, you probably don't have anything new to say on the subject either. Listing the advantages of getting along with each other is also not useful if no one is listening.

Take a deep breath and stay calm. Screeching and screaming only makes you look ridiculous. When you come unglued, the kids only pause long enough to wonder, "What's her problem?" When you're calm, get their attention using the silly, humorous approach. Jason said to his fighting six-year-old son and eight-year-old stepson, "Look, someone dropped dollar bills on the sidewalk." They looked and got caught up in the game of teasing him instead. Other times he jokes, "Oh, I see you're playing 'cats and dogs' again." Such pleasantry puts a less troublesome spin on the rivalry, making it more manageable for both kids and adults.

All kids, whether blood relatives or not, have strong ambivalent feelings toward each other. Letting kids know that it's normal to feel two ways about one another is helpful. Often they don't understand why they're fighting so much either. Jean said to her stepdaughter, "You care about her but right now you're so mad, you want her out of sight."

It's amazing that when you stay calm, the kids work out the most ingenious solutions. Four-year-old Molly and five-year-old Angie were in a tiff over the blue crayon and the coloring book. Mom said, "I see you both want to use the blue crayon and you both want to color the elephant. I think you can find a solution, let me know what you decide." In less than five minutes, the girls were coloring peacefully. "She gets to color the horse blue and I get to color the elephant yellow."

# SOLVE YOUR PROBLEMS
# WITH THEM DIRECTLY

No, they are not *your* children—but they are in your life and therefore you should strive as much as possible to deal with them directly, instead of appealing to their biological parents for help. You want them to see you as one of the adults in their lives whose advice they can benefit from and to whom they can come in times of need, and you can't create that kind of relationship if you are always running to your spouse whenever you have difficulty. To do so is to put yourself on their level—as a child—and place the biological parent over the two of you as the authority figure.

Instead, if you deal directly with them and use the bargaining power you already have, they will begin to realize that you must be taken into account. Sometimes as a stepparent you believe and behave as if you have no bargaining power. Here again you're tempted to look to your spouse for power and authority with the kids. No one can give you personal power, you have to find it within yourself and use what you have. You do have more inner power than you might think.

Lots of stepparents have trouble with this. They sit back and feel abused by their stepkids and resentful that their mate didn't step in to defend them.

Think about where your leverage is. Mark had a flexible work schedule and was willing to drive the kids to their many school activities and social commitments. As long as they were treating him well, he was good-natured, but if they gave him a rough time he wouldn't budge. "You wouldn't help me mow the lawn when I asked so I don't feel like driving you to your friend's house this afternoon." It didn't take long for the kids to learn that cooperating with their stepdad got them more of what they wanted than bucking him.

Think about what you do for the stepkids that is important to them. Do you iron their clothes, lend them your watch, chauffeur their friends, take them fishing, buy them treats? This is where you have power to gain their cooperation. Use your power lightly, without threatening, and you'll have a winning combination.

Will generously took Amanda to the store whenever she asked. "I'll meet you by the front door in thirty minutes," he said. Forty-five minutes later when she still hadn't shown up, he had her paged over the loudspeaker, "Amanda Ford meet your chauffeur at the information counter immediately." Since she didn't like being the focus of attention, that got her out of the store quickly! "Even though she was annoyed," recalled Judy, "I could tell by the slight twinkle in her eye that she had gained appreciation for the fact that she couldn't rattle him. She tested him often but eventually came to understand that he was in charge too, and if she wanted the goodies she'd have to respect his wishes."

# FINE-TUNE YOUR
# SENSE OF HUMOR

This can't be said enough—one of the most important keys to happy stepparenting is to laugh a lot—to yourself, with your mate, and with your stepkids.

"I used to use the 'wicked stepmother' thing a lot when the kids were young," says Anna. "I would say things like, 'Here comes the wicked stepmother to tell you it's time to clean your room,' or 'Here's the wicked stepmother arriving to say you've got to come in for dinner.' It played on the stereotype in such a way that we could all joke about it—and it was remarkably effective in getting them to do as I asked. Because I had called myself the name, they couldn't say it themselves—I usurped any power they might have tried to exert over me by making a joke of it. Because I teased about it, they couldn't take it seriously."

In order to brighten up the daily grind and have closer rapport with your housemates, be willing to laugh at yourself. Yes, it is easier to see the humorous side of your stepchildren and spouse than it is to stand back and see the crazy, immature things you do, but it's worth the effort. If you're willing to laugh at your peculiar little ways, there will be less wear and tear on your nerves.

Learning to laugh with your stepkids and spouse over mistakes and blunders gets things moving in a positive direction more quickly than a somber, serious approach. Laughing at our stepparenting foibles is a creative way, a less hurtful way of problem solving. It gives everyone renewed vigor for cooperating. Admit your blunders, but don't chastise yourself. "Yes, I was behaving like a wild woman last night," said Kate at the parenting group. "After I apologized we all had a good laugh. The next time I'm on the verge of screaming I'll warn the kids, 'Run for cover, the wild woman is taking over.'"

A playful atmosphere is good for all kinds of families; for stepfamilies its an absolute necessity. Blended family life has many comical moments that you can use to turn stone-faced stepkids into chuckling participants. A few laughs a day will keep the stepparenting blahs from strangling the joy. If you can't think of anything funny, or when life is getting dreary, buy a laughing tape and play it as a surprise during dinner. Watch and see what happens.

# DESIGN AN "OUR GANG" ALBUM

W e highly recommend that you design a one-of-a-kind photo and story album to record the history of your expanded family. Just as there are wedding albums, baby books, and vacation albums, we think each stepfamily should have an "Our Gang" album depicting the significant events that makes your clan special. Include the description of your first meeting, record the names of all the relatives in your extended tribe, and display your album in a prominent place so everyone can see it. It's a testimony to your dedication and gives your stepfamily pride and team identification.

We suggest that you buy a scrapbook or a looseleaf notebook to collect treasures and souvenirs. The album, a memento that chronicles your life together, might include an expanded family tree listing *all* the relatives and steprelatives on *all* sides of the family. In drawing the family tree, don't leave anyone out. Even if you don't like them or don't have much to do with them, including them lets you and the kids see how all your lives are intertwined. It reminds everyone that there is no need to be afraid of skeletons in your closets. Another page might show in pictures and words the story of your first meeting, your favorite outing. List your likes and dislikes, your favorite colors, include everyone's little love-names.

Be sure to include plenty of pictures not only of special events like birthdays and Halloween, but of ordinary events such as the step-brothers playing catch together in the backyard, the kids doing chores, or Dad helping with homework. If the kids are old enough, give them a camera and ask them to take pictures of what it's like to be a member of this household.

Include pictures of the kids' biological parents too. Remember the biological parent has a permanent place in your stepchild's heart, so there is no need to stamp them out of the album. That page might be entitled, "Susie's Mother." A word of warning: Be sure to keep the titles upbeat; your stepchildren are highly sensitive to any put-downs of the other parent.

One page might be a statement of your goals: "We want to learn to get along," or "We want to go camping once a month." Write with colorful pens, cut out and paste in inspiring words from magazines to help you reach your goals. Ask the kids if they'd like to contribute. Don't coerce or push them, however. If you're cheerful about the project, they'll be sure to get interested in at least looking it over.

Regardless of what you call it, creating an album with a name, a logo, and a motto accentuates the unseen bond that keeps you hanging in. It's a playful portrayal that keeps you moving upward.

# WATER THE GOOD SEEDS

Vietnamese Buddhist monk Thich Nhat Hahn likes to use the metaphor of a garden when talking about the human personality. Each of us comes into adulthood with a handful of seeds (habits, patterns of feelings, ways of being) that we got from our parents. It is up to us to water the good seeds—seeds of love, compassion, kindness, understanding—so that they can blossom, and let the bad seeds—seeds of anger, despair, envy, fear, judgment—lie fallow. Otherwise we will reap a bitter harvest and pass on the bad seeds to our children.

Those of us who are parents are well aware that the anger and fear we chronically express has a way of showing up in the children in our lives. Many a child has stood between two parents begging them not to fight, only to see themselves saying and doing the exact same things in their adult relationships.

We reap what we sow. Therefore, if we want to live in a happy, loving family, we need to express as much love, compassion, understanding, and kindness to our stepchildren as we possibly can. In doing so, we not only water the good seeds in ourselves but in the children as well. The kinder we are to Lily and Joshua, the more they will learn kindness and live kindness. The angrier, more hostile, and dismissive we are to them, the more they will treat us that way too.

Remember—in planting a garden, there's no such thing as instant results. You have to water again and again before anything begins to emerge. And then the shoots are so tender that the slightest frost can kill them.

The same is true for the loving, tender seeds in our stepchildren. They need a lot of time and attention to grow well, a lot of patient tending. A bit of "frost" from you can do a great deal of damage.

So the next time you've been provoked into saying or doing something out of anger toward them, ask yourself what kind of harvest you want to reap. Water the good seeds in yourself and your stepkids, and your family will eventually become a garden of love.

# LOOK FOR THE
# UNSPOKEN "I LOVE YOU"S

Because our stepchildren may feel conflicted over positive feelings for us—they might feel disloyal to their other parent or resentful over the divorce (and "liking" us might be felt as approval of the split), to name just two reasons—they often have a hard time expressing feelings of love or affection. This can be very hard on us. After all, we pour out a great deal of attention, resources, affection, time, and care toward them—not to mention putting up with having our lives turned upside down—and get very little tangible in return.

In a wonderful book called *Girls Only*, Alex Witchel, a reporter for the *New York Times*, writes about being a stepmother, acknowledging that "you are always the third choice. No matter how much they like you, no one considers you an option for anything until Mom and Dad are unavailable first.... You're taken for granted because you can't be taken too seriously." Still, she points out, stepparenting can be marvelously satisfying and fulfilling, particularly if you look for the "unspoken 'I love you's.'" Because stepkids feel disloyal if they say "I love you" to a stepparent directly, you have to look for all the ways they do say it without words.

For Witchel, it is evident in the way her stepson slowed down to match her pace when she sprained her ankle, while her husband sprinted on ahead, oblivious to her inability to keep up. For Anna it was the way Michael always asked her to read his English and history homework. "He showed me that he knew I was a good writer and could help him." And it was evident in the way Zoe would come into the kitchen around dinnertime whenever she was staying over to ask Anna if there was anything she could do to help. For Erik, it was a letter Candice wrote to him apologizing for giving him a hard time. For Will, it was the way Amanda did her imitation of him. For Cynthia, it was the way her stepson would drape himself on the couch, with always a foot at least somehow touching her. For Margie, it was the way her stepkids would always want to talk to her too when they called home from college.

All of these are the precious rewards of our love and commitment, the sign language our stepkids use to acknowledge that we do matter in their lives. The more we look for such signs, the more we will feel the love that is in their hearts that may be too scary for them to express in any other way. They do care for us—be sure to take the time to notice how.

# WATCH FOR MIRACLES

Just because things might be rocky between you and your stepkids now doesn't mean they will always be that way. If you continue to act in a loving, lighthearted manner, as time goes on, you will become more and more part of their picture of the family. And sometimes, out of the blue, miracles happen.

"Michael was in high school, and we were almost completely alienated. It wasn't open warfare, just a tacit agreement to give one another a wide berth. I was feeling awful. I had been in this child's life for fourteen years, the last four of which he had lived with us full-time, and I felt that we weren't any closer than our first weekend together. I was out of town on a business trip and it happened to be Mother's Day. The phone rang at about 9:00 P.M. in my hotel room. 'I picked up the phone and it was Michael, just calling to wish me Happy Mother's Day.' I was so happy I cried."

Miracles do happen. The child who wished you would drop dead now considers you her best friend; the hostile boy who ignored you for years suddenly calls you Dad; your daughter and hers, who swore eternal enmity, are now running together for class office. You, who've never gotten along well with Joe, suddenly find him funny and entertaining.

Whatever is happening now is not an indication of what the

future will bring, particularly if we leave ourselves open to the possibility of the best outcome. The decision to open our hearts to the stepchildren in our care may need to be made over and over again as time goes by. But as long as we stay open, miracles can happen. The love that you are giving will come back to you somehow—if only in the shape of a child who majors in the same subject as you in college without ever realizing it was because they were so affected by your being in their life.

If you spend any consistent amount of time with a child, you will have a profound effect on who they are, and what matters to them in the world. Your existence in this child's life, this child who so "randomly" and "unintentionally" ended up with you, will help them become who they are meant to be. Isn't *that* miracle enough?

# NO MATTER WHAT, HOLD THEIR SOULS IN THE LIGHT

$A$bove all, when things are rough, remember that these are young souls that have been entrusted to your care. You have a profound responsibility, a sacred duty, to help these souls blossom into their unique fullness. Even if today is full of argument and tension, you can hold the intention that tomorrow will be better and that these souls will find, with your help, the love and peace they are so hungry for.

Never underestimate the power of loving prayers to effect a good outcome. One prayer we like to say, especially when we are having trouble with someone, is called the "loving-kindness meditation." You start with yourself: may I be peaceful; may I be happy; may I be free from suffering; may I be filled with loving kindness. You then go to anyone you are having trouble with and offer them the same blessing: may Susie be peaceful; may Susie be happy; may Susie be free from suffering; may Susie be filled with loving-kindness. You then continue doing it for as many people as you want.

No matter what else is going on, the spiritual connection between us and our stepchildren is always there; when you pray, your souls will be linking up in some ineffable way. Even if it doesn't cause Susie to be nicer, we've noticed that it helps us to be nicer to Susie, which in turn ripples back to us.

Children come into our lives in many different ways—through birth; through adoption and fostering; and through stepfamilies. No matter how they got here, they are now a part of us and we a part of them. By a "twist of fate," your soul and the soul of your stepchild are now forever linked. When we acknowledge that link, when we see our task as caretaker of this budding soul, it is much easier to rise above the small stuff and focus on what truly matters. May we love them well—and may we have some fun in the process.

# Resource Guide

## STEPPARENTING

**Stepfamily Association of America**
215 Centennial Mall South
Suite 212
Lincoln, NE 68508
www.stepfam.org
800-735-0329

**Stepfamily Foundation**
333 West End Avenue
New York, NY 10023
(212) 877-3244
24-hour crisis line:
(212) 799-STEP

**The Joint Custody Association**
10606 Wilkins Avenue
Los Angeles, CA 90024
(310) 475-5352

**Positive Steps**
An online support group for
stepfamilies
www.postivesteps.com.

## WORK AND FAMILY ISSUES

**Families and Work Institute**
330 Seventh Avenue
New York, NY 10001
(212) 465-2044

**The Family Resource Center**
3041 Olcott Street
Santa Clara, CA 95054-3222

**Full-time Dads Newsletter**
http://www.parentsplace.com/rea
droom/fulltdad

Children's Rights Council
220 I Street N.E.
Suite 230
Washington, DC 20002-4362

**SPECIFIC ISSUES**
**Exceptional Parents**
For parents with disabilities
1 800-247-8080

**National Information Center
    for Children and Youth with
    Disabilities**
1 800-695-0285

**Resource Center on Child Abuse
    and Neglect**
63 Inverness Drive East
Englewood, CO 8012X
(303) 792-9900
800-227-5242

**Momazons**
National referral network for
    lesbian mothers
(614) 267-0193

**MOMS Club**
For at-home mothers
25371 Rye Canyon Road
Valencia, CA 91355

**Mothers of Preschoolers**
311 South Clarkson Street
Denver, CO 80210
(303) 733-5353

**Mothers At Home**
8310A Old Courthouse Road
Vienna, Virginia 22182
800-783-4666
E-mail: MAH@netrail.net

**National Committee to Prevent
    Child Abuse**
32 South Michigan Avenue
Chicago, IL 60604
(312) 663-3520
800-CHILDREN

**American Anorexia/Bulimia
    Association**
(212) 891-8686

National Association of Anorexia
   Nervosa
(708) 831-3438

Family Violence Prevention Fund
800-313-1310

National Runaway Switchboard
800-621-4000

National Youth Crisis Hotline
800-448-4663

Rape, Abuse, and Incest National
   Network
800-656-4673

Alcohol and Drug Helpline
800-821-4357

Cocaine Helpline
800-262-2463

National Clearinghouse for
   Alcohol and Drug Information
800-729-6686

National Child Safety Council
   Childwatch
800-222-1464

National AIDS Hotline
800-342-2437

Depression Awareness,
   Recognition, and Treatment
800-421-4211

National Foundation for
   Depressive Illness
800-245-4381

National Clearinghouse on Family
   Support and Children's Mental
   Health
800-628-1696

Planned Parenthood Federation of
   America, Inc.
800-669-0156

## Books by Judy Ford

*Wonderful Ways to Love a Child*

*Wonderful Ways to Love a Teen... Even When It Seems Impossible*

*Blessed Expectations: Nine Months of Wonder,*
*Reflection & Sweet Anticipation*

*Wonderful Ways to Love a Grandchild*

*Wonderful Ways to Be a Family*

For information on
Judy Ford's workshops and presentations write:
P.O. Box 834
Kirkland, WA 98083
425-823-4421

E-mail:
JFORDBOOKS@aol.com

Conari Press, established in 1987, publishes books
on topics ranging from psychology, spirituality, and women's
history to sexuality, parenting, and personal growth.
Our main goal is to publish quality books that will make a
difference in people's lives—both how we feel
about ourselves and how we relate
to one another.

Our readers are our most important resource,
and we value your input, suggestions, and ideas.
We'd love to hear from you—after all, we are
publishing books for you!

To request our latest book catalog,
or to be added to our mailing list, please contact:

CONARI PRESS
2550 Ninth Street, Suite 101
Berkeley, California 94710-2551
800-685-9595 • 510-649-7175
fax: 510-649-7190
E-mail: Conaripub@aol.com